RETURN TO FACTOPia!

Follow the TRAIL of 400 MORE FACTS

BY KATE HALE

Illustrated by ANDY SMITH

BRITANNICA
BOOKS

Contents

Welcome back to FACTopia!

It's time to set off on another adventure through hundreds of mind-blowing, wow-worthy, and crazily cool facts. For example...

Did you know that astronauts have played golf on the Moon?

Let's blast off with astronauts! They can actually grow taller while they're in space.

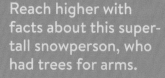

Reach higher with facts about this super-tall snowperson, who had trees for arms.

And trees aren't just for decoration—in forests they actually talk to one another through a network of fungi, called the Wood Wide Web.

Speaking of fungi, did you know there's a fungus that glows in the dark?

You might have spotted that there is something special about being here in FACTopia. Every fact is *linked to the next*, and in the most surprising and even hilarious ways.

You will follow a trail that takes you from **toilets** to **ice cream** to **chili peppers** to **ancient Egypt** to **tug-of-war** to the **Moon** to... well, you'll see. Discover what each turn of the page will bring!

But there isn't just one trail through this book. Your path branches every now and then, and you can **flip backward** or **leap forward** to go to a totally different (*but still connected*) part of FACTopia.

Let your curiosity take you wherever it leads.
Of course, a good place to start could be right here, at the beginning.

For example, take this detour to find out about really jumpy things

Go to page 170

...The Sun rises only once per year at the

NORTH

Brighten up!

POLE

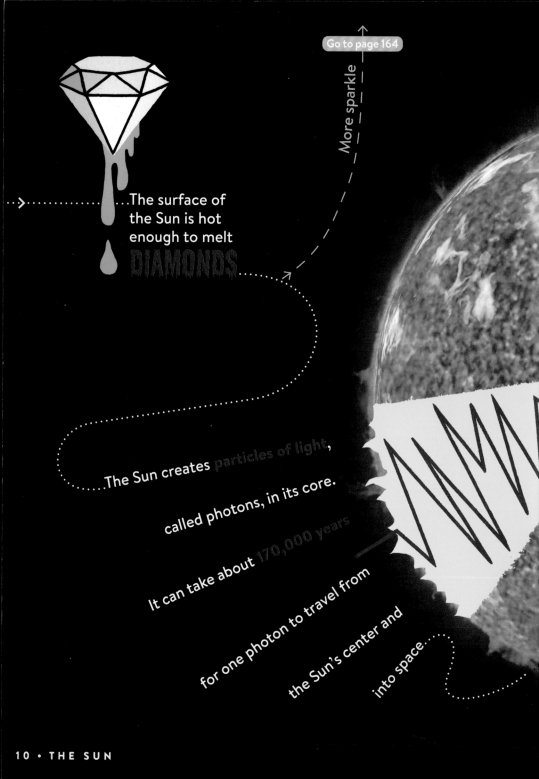

Go to page 164

More sparkle

The surface of the Sun is hot enough to melt DIAMONDS

The Sun creates particles of light, called photons, in its core.

It can take about 170,000 years for one photon to travel from the Sun's center and into space...

About every 11 years, the Sun's north and south poles swap places. This change causes the Northern Lights on Earth to become more active.

Look up!

Some people can hear the Northern Lights

Go to page 142

I'm all ears!

Brrr!

At one hotel in the Arctic, guest rooms are **glass igloos**, so you can better view the Northern Lights

Go to page 72

Fly on over here!

Polar bears have black skin under their fur

Bird poop helps keep
the Arctic cool.
It creates gases that
help form clouds, which
reflect light from the
Sun back into space.

Ice in the Arctic Ocean can be as thick as **10 mattresses** stacked on top of one another...

Narwhals, found in the Arctic Ocean, can have a long, pointed tooth that's earned them the nickname "**unicorns of the sea.**" Some narwhals even have two...

The tip of the iceberg

Icy structures called **frost flowers** can form on Arctic sea ice. These delicate formations are three times saltier than the ocean and home to millions of microscopic organisms.

Scientists believe that about 715 million years ago Earth may have been entirely covered in ice in what's called the **Snowball** Earth theory.

There's an international **snowball**-fighting championship held in Japan each year. It takes place in a snow field at the base of a **volcano**.

There's a tiny amount of **gold** in every **cell phone**.

The average **cell phone** has up to 10 times more germs than a **toilet** seat.

A jeweler once created a version of the **game** Monopoly that was worth $2 million. The dice had diamonds instead of dots and the board was made of **gold**.

Hogwarts, the fictional **castle** from the Harry Potter book series, has 142 **staircases**.

A **toilet** in a medieval **castle** was called a garderobe.

The world's longest **staircase**, with 11,674 steps, is built on a **mountain** in Switzerland.

The dust emitted from one of the most powerful **volcano** eruptions on Earth caused the Moon to appear **blue**.

Blue **whales** can communicate with one another from 1,000 miles (1,609km) apart.

Scientists can tell how old a **whale** is from its **earwax**.

Cerumen, the medical term for **earwax**, isn't actually wax at all—it's a combination of skin cells, **sweat**, dirt, and a fatty substance called sebum that your body makes.

Some football players can **sweat** up to 9 pounds (4kg) of fluid during a **game**.

Mauna Kea in Hawaii is actually the tallest **mountain** on Earth. It's more than 1 mile (1.6km) taller than Everest, but most of it is submerged under the **ocean**.

Over thousands of years **ocean** waves can create sea caves. Some caves even have blowholes, where water sprays out of a small hole in the roof.

Head inside!

One of the chambers in the **world's largest cave** is so big it could fit an entire city block, complete with 40-story skyscrapers, inside......

Bracken Cave in Texas is home to the world's largest known **bat colony**—it can take up to four hours for all 20 million bats to fly out of the cave each night

Go batty!

Some species of bat can eat 1,000 insects in a single hour...

There are over **1.5 million Mexican free-tailed bats** that live for

Go to page 70

Juicy!

Baby bats are called pups.

Get the scoop on poop!

Not all bats eat insects. Some eat seeds, pollen, and fruit.

When bats eat a lot of chitin (the shiny material that insect bodies are made of), their poop sparkles.

part of the year underneath a bridge in Austin, Texas

An avocado is a

BERRY

Pink pearl apples have **bright pink flesh.**

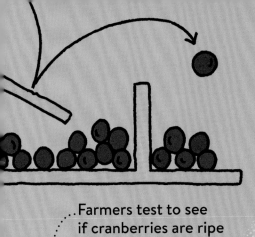

Farmers test to see if cranberries are ripe by **bouncing** them...

Grow on!

.The small "seeds" on the outside of a strawberry aren't actually seeds at all, they're **fruits**! Each one has a tiny seed inside...

...The durian is a fruit so **smelly** that *it's* banned on Singapore's public transit system...

The world's largest seed, from the Coco de Mer fruit, can weigh more than two bowling balls.

SVALBARD GLOBAL SEED VAULT

The
Svalbard
Global Seed
Vault, located
inside a mountain
in Norway and designed
to withstand global disasters,
contains more than **one million** seed samples.

Time to bloom →

For a brief time in Holland's history, some tulips cost more than houses

Broccoli is a flower

More sunshine

Go to page 10

In Victorian times, people used flowers to pass messages in a language called

FLORIOGRAPHY.

A rhododendron meant danger, a daisy meant innocence, and ivy or acacia meant friendship.

Buzzzzz

Some flower species smell like **chocolate**

Young sunflowers move their heads through the day so that they always **face the Sun**—at night they reset, ready for sunrise

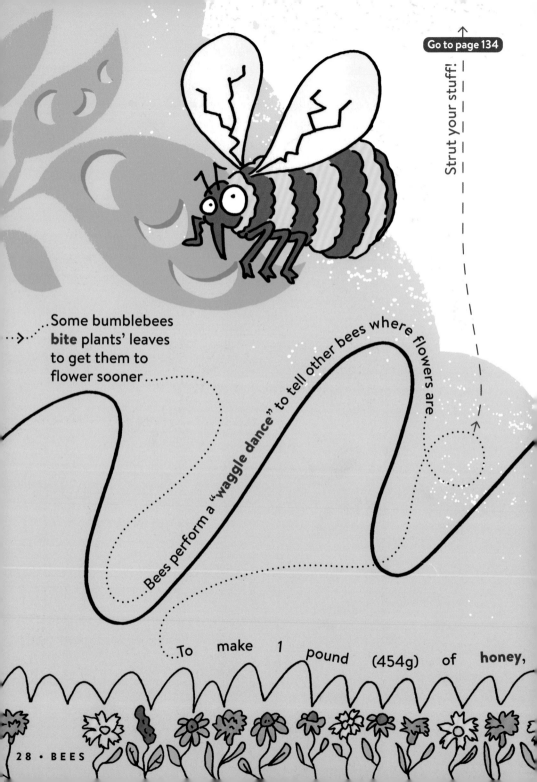

Go to page 134

Strut your stuff!

Some bumblebees **bite** plants' leaves to get them to flower sooner

Bees perform a "waggle dance" to tell other bees where flowers are

To make 1 pound (454g) of **honey,**

Sweet!

honeybees need to visit about **two million flowers.**

Bees can sometimes make honey without flower nectar. Some bees in France made honey after eating pieces of M&Ms—the honey was blue and green.

Archaeologists have found honey in **ancient Egyptian tombs** that's still edible despite being thousands of years old.

Dig up some more!

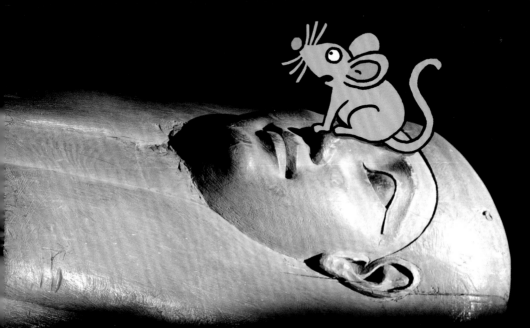

Purr-fect

After their **pet cats** died, ancient Egyptians sometimes mummified them......

One musician **composed songs specifically for cats**. The music includes squeaks, birdlike chirping, and even purring...

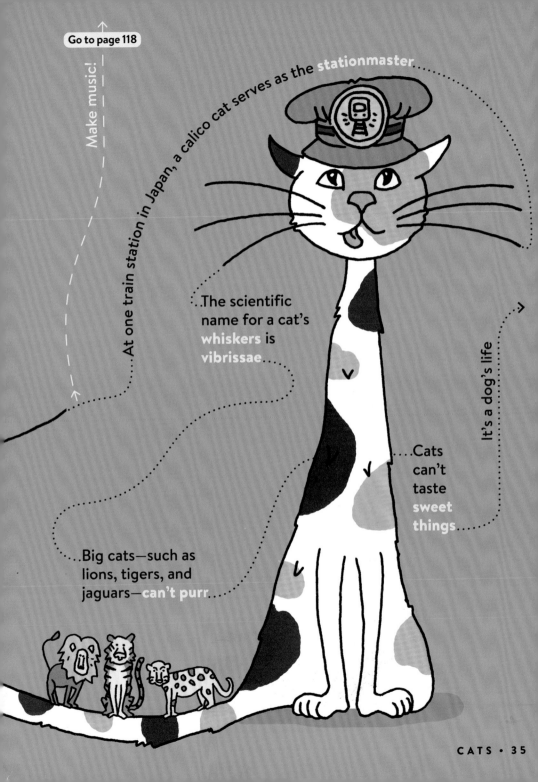

Go to page 118

Make music!

At one train station in Japan, a calico cat serves as the **stationmaster**

.The scientific name for a cat's **whiskers** is **vibrissae**.

It's a dog's life

.Cats can't taste **sweet things**.

.Big cats—such as lions, tigers, and jaguars—**can't purr**.

Yawning is contagious—even between dogs and their owners.

Dalmatian puppies are born **completely white**—their spots develop only as they grow up.

A dog's **paws** are the only parts of its body that sweat.

Some restaurants have **special menus** for dogs—one in California features hot dogs, hamburger patties, and even a "good dog" steak....

Feeling hungry?

Dogs DREAM

There's a restaurant where you eat dinner on a table suspended 165 feet (50m) in the air...

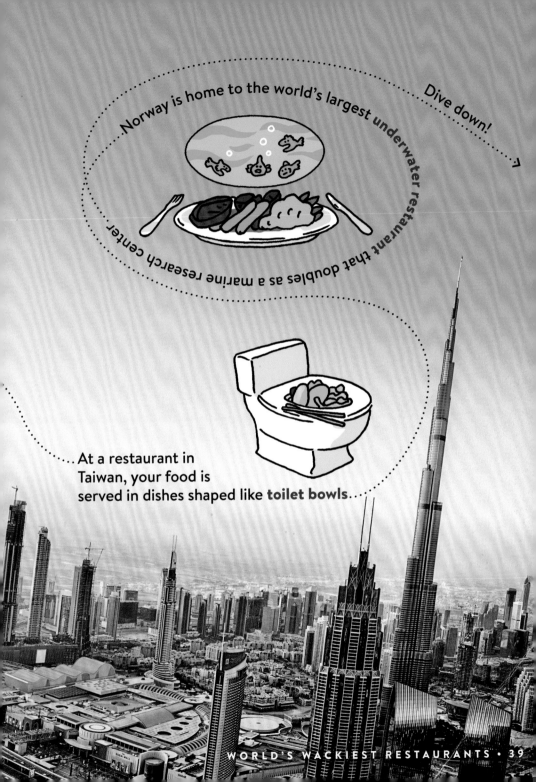

Dive down!

Norway is home to the world's largest underwater restaurant that doubles as a marine research center

At a restaurant in Taiwan, your food is served in dishes shaped like **toilet bowls**

In 1992, 28,000 bath toys, including rubber ducks, beavers, and

...The world's largest waterfall is underneath the ocean—2,000 times more water flows over it than over Niagara Falls...

...The deepest-swimming fish are snailfish, which can live 5 miles (8km) below the ocean's surface—that's so deep the water pressure could crush human bone...

Falling water

Go to page 180

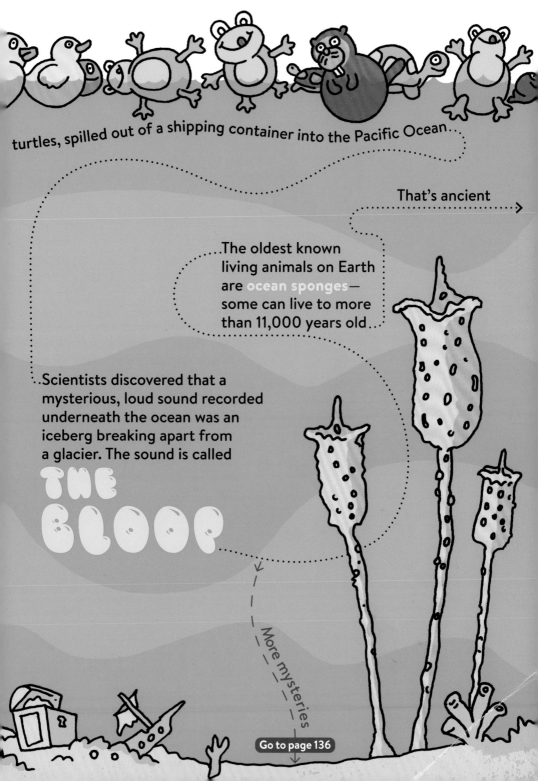

turtles, spilled out of a shipping container into the Pacific Ocean...

That's ancient

The oldest known living animals on Earth are ocean sponges— some can live to more than 11,000 years old...

Scientists discovered that a mysterious, loud sound recorded underneath the ocean was an iceberg breaking apart from a glacier. The sound is called

THE BLOOP

More mysteries

Go to page 136

Methuselah is a 5,000-year-old bristlecone pine growing in California—the tree is older than the pyramids of ancient Egypt.

Twice a year at the Mayan pyramid of Kukulcán in Mexico, the Sun casts a shadow that looks like a giant slithering snake.

Some beaches have pink sand because the grains are actually shells of microscopic marine animals.

Saturn's rings are made of ice and rock—some chunks are only as big as a grain of sand, others are the size of a mountain.

Scientists think Mars used to have a set of rings around it.

The two shells of a giant clam can weigh about 550 pounds (250kg)—that's more than two adult giant pandas.

People in ancient Ireland buried butter in swampy wetlands called bogs, which helped preserve the food.

At birth, baby giant pandas weigh about the same as a stick of butter.

Adult ankylosaurs had club-like **tails**, the impact of which was more than 350 times stronger than the hit from a professional **baseball** player's bat.

Scientists can identify individual anaconda **snakes** by the scale pattern underneath their **tails**—no two are the same.

Every **baseball** used in an American professional league game is rubbed with special **mud** collected from a secret spot in New Jersey.

There's a **crater** on **Mars** that's nicknamed "happy face" because it looks like it's smiling.

You can take a **mud** bath inside the **crater** of a volcano in Colombia.

Every year, Wales, U.K., holds the World **Bog** Snorkelling Championship, in which competitors swim through muddy water wearing snorkels, **flippers**, and sometimes wacky costumes.

The **flippers** of humpback whales aren't smooth— they're bumpy. Scientists have been studying these bumps, called tubercles, to make more aerodynamic airplane wings.

It's a whale of a fact

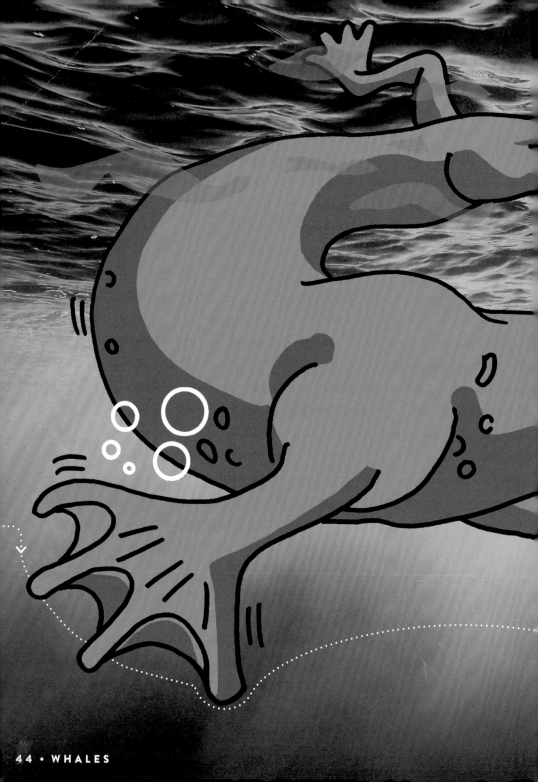

Back in time

One species of ancient whale had **four legs** and webbed feet

Go to page 150

Go bananas!

Some saber-toothed cats had fangs the size of bananas. Scientists also think they drooled.

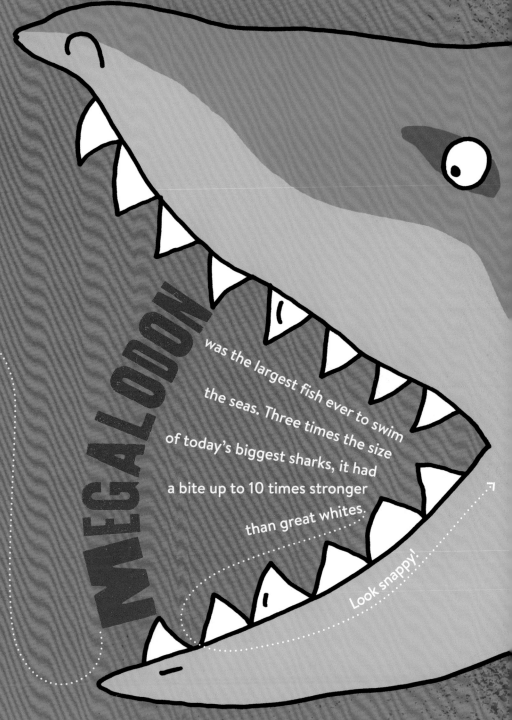

MEGALODON was the largest fish ever to swim the seas. Three times the size of today's biggest sharks, it had a bite up to 10 times stronger than great whites.

Look snappy!

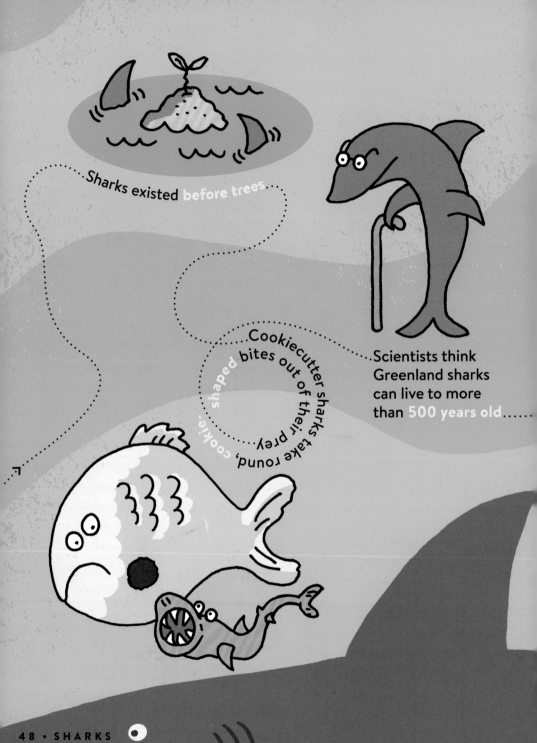

Sharks existed before trees.

Cookiecutter sharks take round, cookie-shaped bites out of their prey.

Scientists think Greenland sharks can live to more than 500 years old......

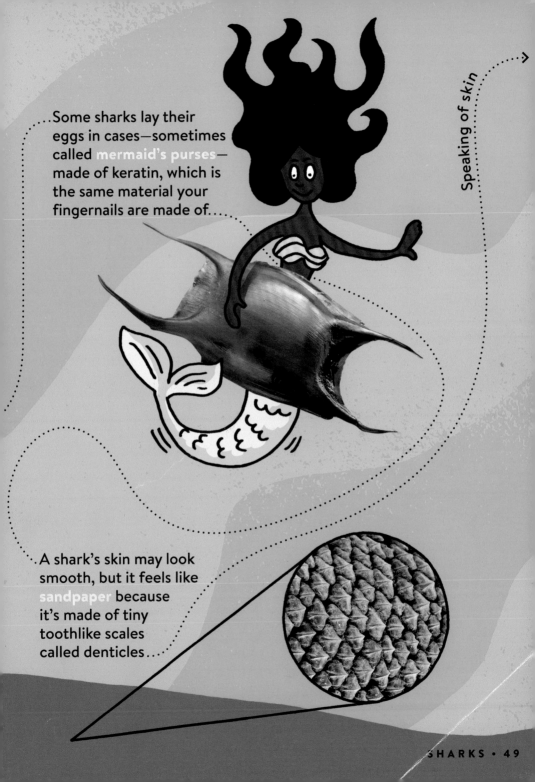

Some sharks lay their eggs in cases—sometimes called **mermaid's purses**— made of keratin, which is the same material your fingernails are made of.

A shark's skin may look smooth, but it feels like **sandpaper** because it's made of tiny toothlike scales called denticles.

....If you **weighed** all the skin on an average adult's body, it would equal about 8 pounds (3.6kg)—that's heavier than a Yorkshire terrier.

Frogs can **breathe** through their skin...

Go to page 170

Hop on over!

It's not only a tiger's fur that's striped—its

SKIN

is striped, too...

Blend in!

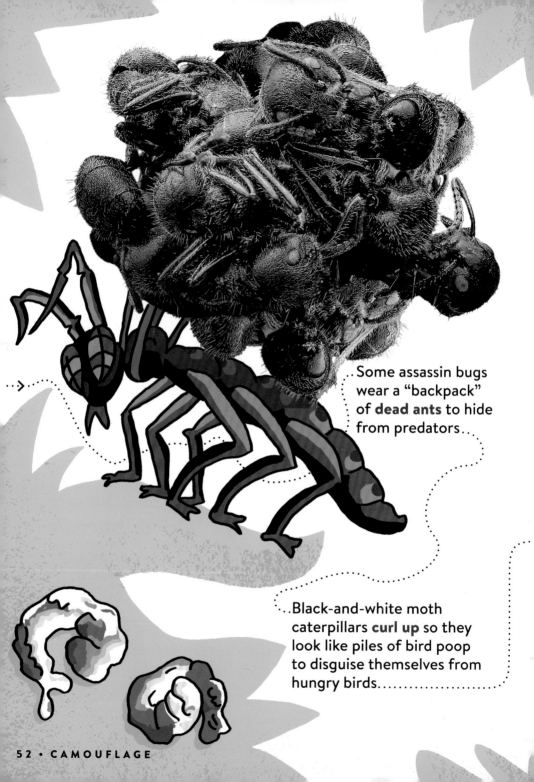

Some assassin bugs wear a "backpack" of **dead ants** to hide from predators.

Black-and-white moth caterpillars **curl up** so they look like piles of bird poop to disguise themselves from hungry birds.

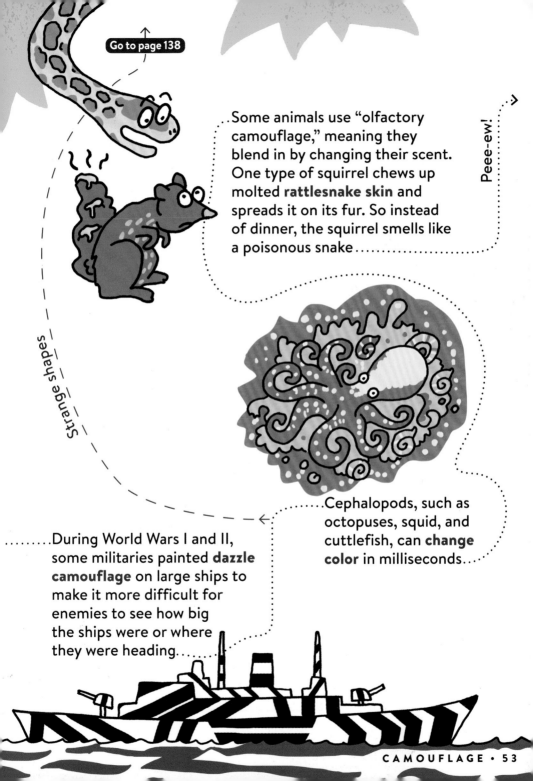

Go to page 138

Some animals use "olfactory camouflage," meaning they blend in by changing their scent. One type of squirrel chews up molted **rattlesnake skin** and spreads it on its fur. So instead of dinner, the squirrel smells like a poisonous snake

Peee-ew!

Strange shapes

Cephalopods, such as octopuses, squid, and cuttlefish, can **change color** in milliseconds.

During World Wars I and II, some militaries painted **dazzle camouflage** on large ships to make it more difficult for enemies to see how big the ships were or where they were heading.

Some sharks can smell

BLOOD

from up to a quarter
of a mile (0.4km) away.

...Scents can **trigger memories** because your sense of smell is tied to systems in your brain responsible for emotion and memory.

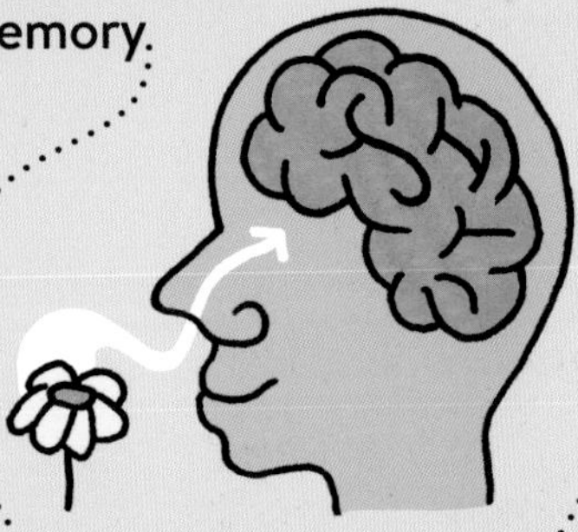

Mind-blowing

Sharks lurking

Go to page 48

The human brain creates enough electricity to power a small light bulb.

↑
Go to page 156

Zap!

Jellyfish

have no brains...

More tentacles this way

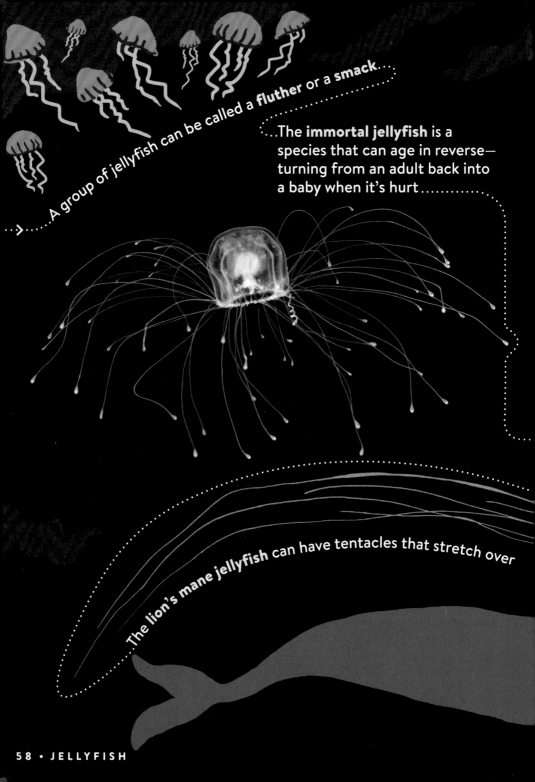

A group of jellyfish can be called a **fluther** or a **smack**.

...The **immortal jellyfish** is a species that can age in reverse— turning from an adult back into a baby when it's hurt...

The **lion's mane jellyfish** can have tentacles that stretch over

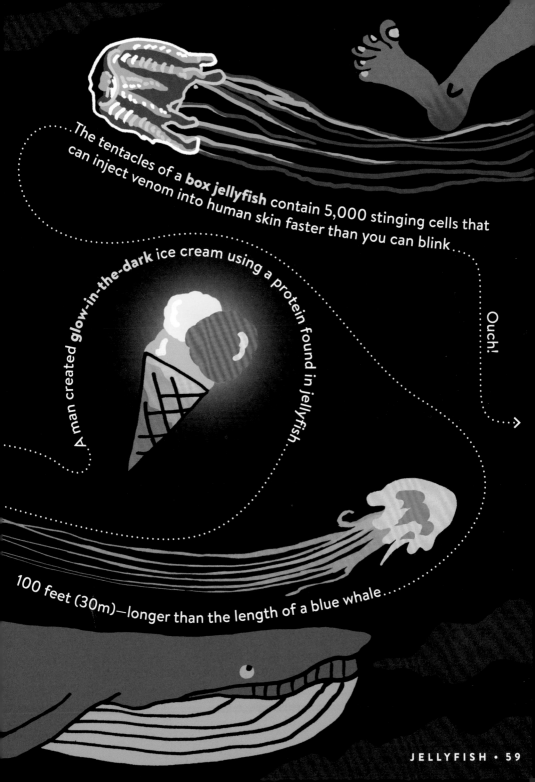

The tentacles of a **box jellyfish** contain 5,000 stinging cells that can inject venom into human skin faster than you can blink.

Ouch!

A man created **glow-in-the-dark** ice cream using a protein found in jellyfish.

100 feet (30m)—longer than the length of a blue whale.

African crested rats have **deadly fur**—they chew toxic tree bark into a paste and spread the poisonous mixture onto themselves.

Emerald jewel wasps inject **mind-control venom** into cockroaches' brains.

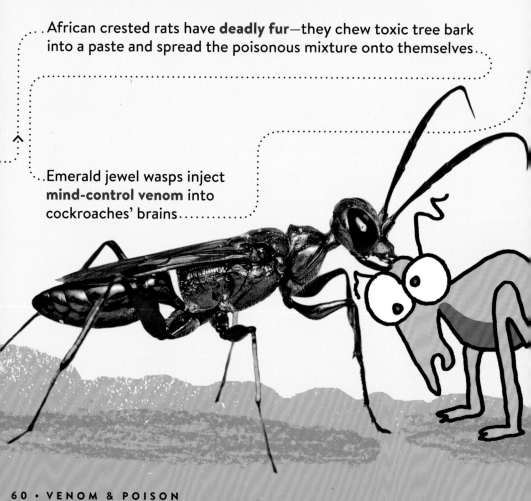

No people live on Snake Island, off the coast of Brazil, because it is home to thousands of golden lancehead vipers, whose venom can **melt human flesh**.......

Sssslither on!

Garter snakes are **social reptiles**—they have friends

There are five species of **flying snake**—these don't technically fly, but glide from tree to

The Barbados threadsnake is the world's **smallest serpent**—it's only as wide as a piece of spaghetti

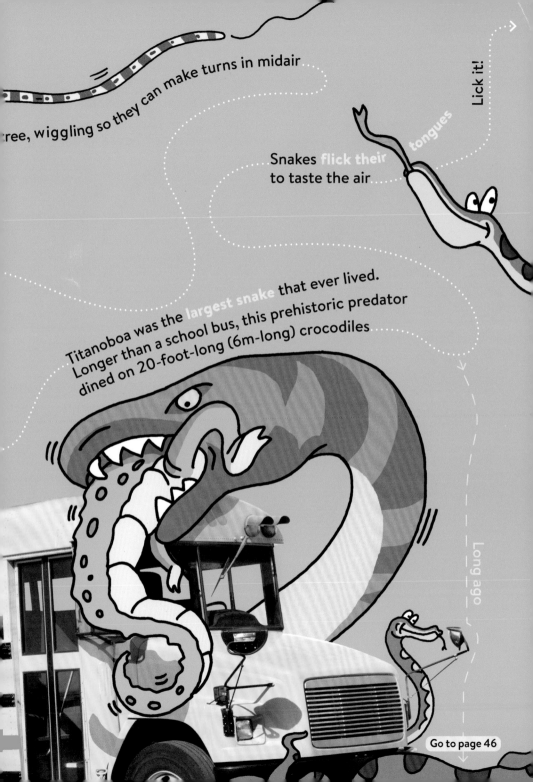

...ree, wiggling so they can make turns in midair

Snakes **flick their** tongues to taste the air...

Lick it!

Titanoboa was the **largest snake** that ever lived. Longer than a school bus, this prehistoric predator dined on 20-foot-long (6m-long) crocodiles...

Long ago

Go to page 46

A pangolin's tongue stretches all the way through its body to its rear end

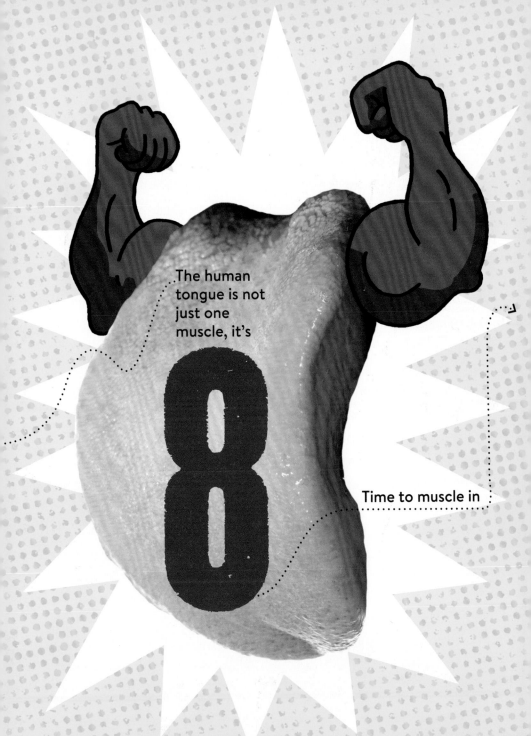

The human tongue is not just one muscle, it's

8

Time to muscle in

If you can control your auricular muscles you can wiggle your ears.

There are no muscles inside your fingers.

The biggest muscle in your body is in your bottom

It's behind you!

Scientists once thought some dinosaurs had a **second brain** located near their rear ends.

Time for number two

A beaver produces a substance near its butt that smells like **vanilla**—sometimes it's used in perfumes.

The wombat is the only animal in the world whose poop is cube-shaped

The **white part** of bird poop is not actually poop—it's bird pee.

Go to page 104

Blast off!

Tweet tweet!

Astronauts have left bags of poop on the Moon.

The **bright pink poop** from some Adélie penguin colonies can be seen from space.

The white sand on Hawaii's beaches is poop from **parrotfish**. The fish eat coral, which get ground up inside them and come out the other end.

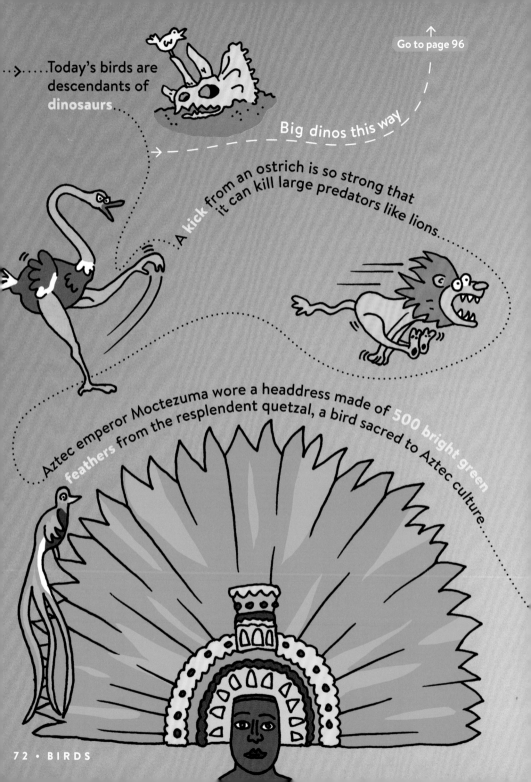

↑
Go to page 96

..>.....Today's birds are descendants of **dinosaurs**.

Big dinos this way

A kick from an ostrich is so strong that it can kill large predators like lions....

Aztec emperor Moctezuma wore a headdress made of 500 bright green feathers from the resplendent quetzal, a bird sacred to Aztec culture....

Sociable weaver birds build huge nests that are like **apartment complexes**—one nest can have more than 100 rooms, each for a different weaver family.

No place like home

Baby European roller birds spit orange vomit in the faces of predators...

The world's only toilet-shaped house is in South Korea. Today it's a museum and features toilet-themed art on the grounds, including a golden pile of poop

Lift the lid!

In the 16th century, tending to the king of England while he used the toilet was a prestigious **job** known as the "Groom of the Stool."

You can get a **job** as a professional **ice cream** taster.

The ancient Greeks believed **onions** made them stronger and ate them while training for the **Olympics**.

In **ancient Egypt**, a mummy's eyes were sometimes replaced with **onions**.

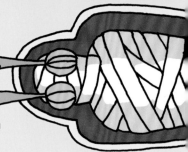

Tug-of-war was once an **Olympic sport**.

One **ice cream** shop sells a flavor called "Cold Sweat"—it's made with three types of **chili pepper** and two different hot sauces.

The chemical found in **chili peppers**, capsaicin, is used in some **medicines** to relieve pain.

Moldy bread and honey were used as **medicines** in **ancient Egypt**.

Golf is the only **sport** that's ever been played on the **Moon**.

There are mirrors on the **Moon**. Scientists on Earth shoot lasers at the mirrors to take measurements.

Time to reflect

The Hall of Mirrors in France's **Palace of Versailles** has 357 mirrors.

The fairytale *Snow White* may have been inspired by a **German baroness** whose family owned a mirror factory.

Some animals, such as **chimpanzees, elephants, and magpies,** can recognize themselves in a mirror.

Smarty-pants!

such as
elephants,
an recognize
a mirror.

An African gray parrot named Alex was **trained to count** and also understand the concept of zero, something most humans don't understand until age four.

Chimpanzees perform better than humans on some **memory tests**.

Aping around

When it rains, an orangutan will sometimes use a **large leaf** as an **umbrella**

There are **four types** of great ape:

1.
CHIMPANZEES

2.
GORILLAS

3.
BONOBOS

4.
ORANGUTANS

Some scientists classify humans as great apes, too.

Unlike all other apes, bonobo groups are matriarchal, meaning that their **leaders are female**

Mountain gorillas **live in forests** located at the same altitudes that **skydivers** reach to jump from planes

Fasten your seatbelt! ····>

Chimpanzees make **laughing noises** when tickled

Go to page 158

Lightning-quick

Airplanes are designed to withstand **lightning strikes**. On average, passenger planes are hit by one lIghtning bolt per year.

....The plane with the world's **largest wingspan** stretches wider than a football field. It won't actually carry passengers, but rockets that launch satellites into space.............

Flap your wings!

Food tastes different on an airplane: The dry air in the cabin combined with the flying altitude makes your taste buds about 30 percent less sensitive to **sweet and salty** foods.

Time to fly ⋯⋯⋯⟩

Andean condors rarely flap their wings while flying. Scientists recorded one bird that soared for over 100 miles (160km) without flapping its wings once

Common swiftlets can fly for nearly a year straight without ever landing on the **ground**.

Some types of **cloud** can weigh more than 1 million pounds (500,000kg)— that's the same as 71 **African elephants**.

Scientists have found a **water cloud** in space that could fill Earth's oceans 140 trillion times.

An **African elephant**'s trunk has 40,000 **muscles**—humans have only about 650 muscles in their entire body.

Scientists have made artificial **muscles** out of the type of plastic used in **potato chip** bags.

When rain hits the **ground**, a type of bacteria releases a chemical called geosmin that gives off an earthy scent. Some people bottle it for **perfumes!**

Some **perfumes** include an ingredient called ambergris, a substance made in the intestines of **sperm whales**.

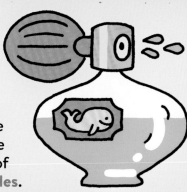

Sperm whales have the biggest brains of any animal on Earth—six times larger than the **human brain**.

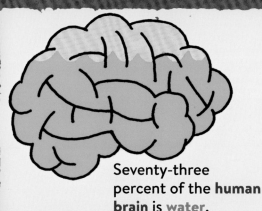

Seventy-three percent of the **human brain** is **water**.

The largest **potato chip** bag ever made weighed 2,515 pounds (1,141kg) and was nearly as tall as a house—it contained sea-salt-flavored chips.

That's record-breaking

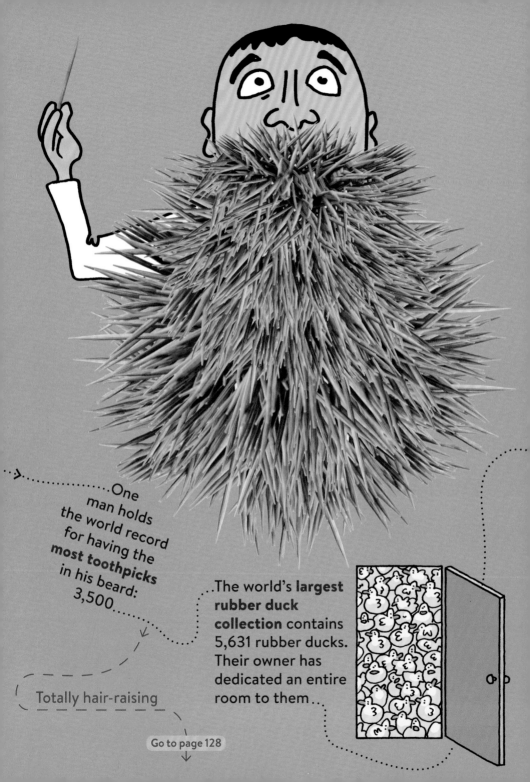

One man holds the world record for having the **most toothpicks** in his beard: 3,500.

Totally hair-raising

Go to page 128

The world's **largest rubber duck collection** contains 5,631 rubber ducks. Their owner has dedicated an entire room to them.

Go to page 98

What's the score?

Bini holds a world record for **most basketball slam dunks** made by a rabbit in one minute: seven

Finley, a golden retriever from Canada, holds a world record for fitting the **most tennis balls** in his mouth at once: six

Teeny-tiny facts

The world's **smallest sculpture** of a teddy bear is smaller than the tiniest ant on Earth.

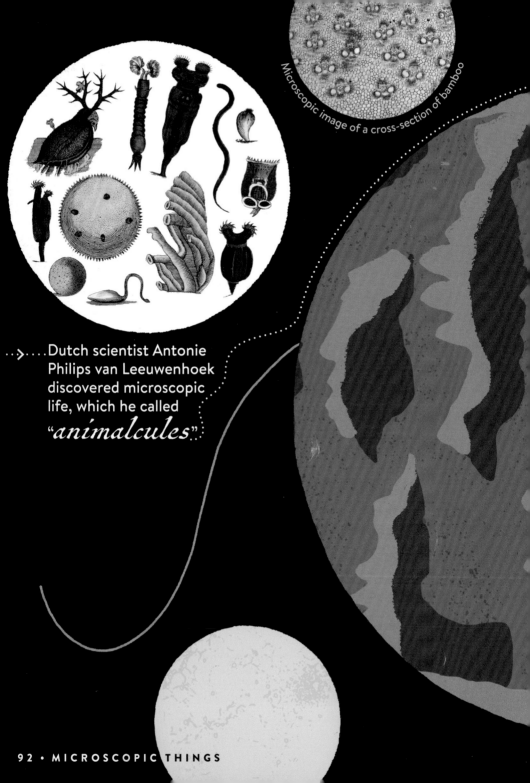

Microscopic image of a cross-section of bamboo

..>....Dutch scientist Antonie
Philips van Leeuwenhoek
discovered microscopic
life, which he called
"*animalcules*"

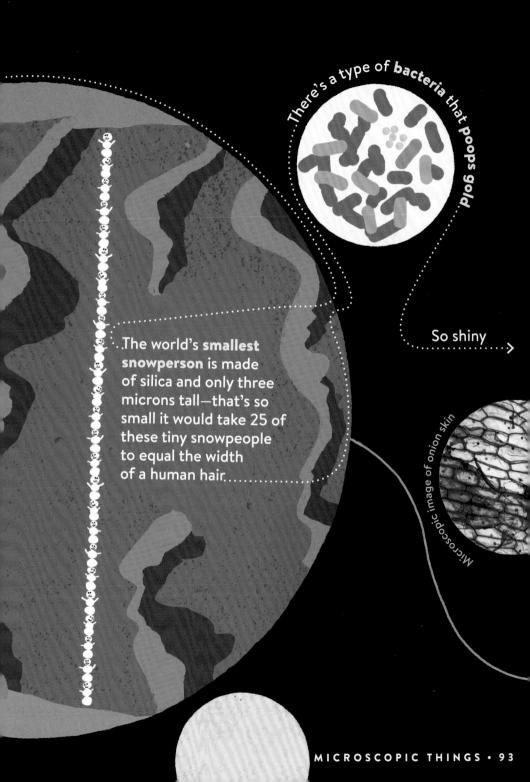

There's a type of **bacteria** that poops gold

So shiny →

The world's **smallest snowperson** is made of silica and only three microns tall—that's so small it would take 25 of these tiny snowpeople to equal the width of a human hair.

Microscopic image of onion skin

When **astronauts** eject their poop from the International Space Station, the poop burns up in Earth's atmosphere and can look like a shooting **star**.

There is a layer of gold on an **astronaut's** helmet.

The number of **stars** in the universe is equal to the number of molecules in just 10 drops of **water**.

Volcanoes can erupt with magma that contains **diamonds**—the last one known to have occurred on Earth was about 25 million years ago.

Some **sharks** live inside underwater **volcanoes**.

Scientists recently discovered the only known **plant**-eating species of **shark**.

Paleontologists have found 2.7-billion-year-old-**raindrop** impressions that became **fossils**.

Diamond **raindrops** that can weigh millions of carats fall on Neptune and Uranus.

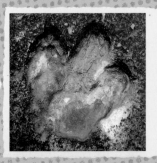

The Australian water-holding frog can store enough water throughout its body that it doesn't need to drink for several years.

The Goliath frog is the world's largest frog—it can weigh as much as a house cat.

Bamboo is the world's fastest-growing plant. Some species can grow 3 feet (1m) in a day.

Cats have more bones than the average adult human.

Giant pandas have special wrist bones that help them grip bamboo.

The dinosaur Tyrannosaurus rex could eat 500 pounds (227kg) of meat in one bite—that's the same as 2,000 hamburgers!

Fossils of dinosaur footprints are called ichnites.

More dino-discovery

Tyrannosaurus rex (*T. rex*) had **holes in its skull** to help keep its brain cool.

A baby *T. rex* was only about the size of a **Chihuahua**.

Go to page 56 ↑

Brainiac facts this way

"Scotty" is the largest T. rex ever discovered. At more than 19,000 pounds (8,600kg), the dinosaur would have weighed nearly as much as **five rhinos**

Get sporty!

Some humans could have **outrun a T. rex**

Tyrannosaurus rex combines the **Greek and Latin** words for

"KING OF THE TYRANT LIZARDS"

In the first tennis matches, people hit the ball with the palm of their hand instead of a racket.

Famous baseball player Babe Ruth sometimes put a cabbage leaf under his hat to stay cool.

Eat your greens!

PAINTING, WRITING,& SCULPTURE

were once Olympic events.

The state of Alaska is known for growing giant, **record-breaking** vegetables—like 138-pound (63kg) cabbages—because the Sun shines there about 20 hours a day every summer...

Austria's Vegetable Orchestra plays concerts with **instruments** made out of vegetables, such as leek violins, carrot marimbas, and pepper trumpets...

Drumroll, please

Go to page 118

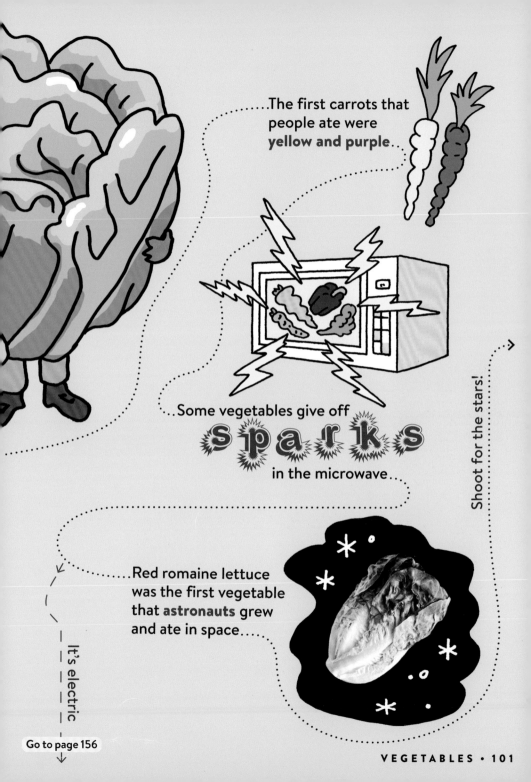

...The first carrots that people ate were **yellow and purple**.

Some vegetables give off **sparks** in the microwave.

Shoot for the stars!

...Red romaine lettuce was the first vegetable that **astronauts** grew and ate in space....

It's electric

Go to page 156

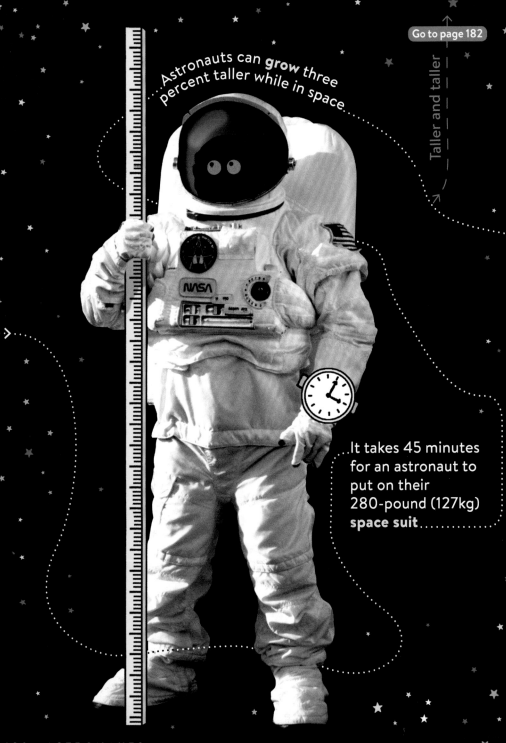

Astronauts can **grow three percent taller** while in space.

Go to page 182

Taller and taller

It takes 45 minutes for an astronaut to put on their 280-pound (127kg) **space suit**

On the International Space Station, most astronauts **sleep** in compartments about the size of a phone booth.

Some astronauts say that space **smells** like burning steak, gunpowder, and raspberries. The smell has even been recreated and turned into a perfume.

The **footprints** that astronauts left on the Moon could last for millions of years because there is no wind to disturb them.

Over the Moon!

The **MOON** is shrinking.

Earth's oldest rock was discovered on the Moon. Scientists think it landed there after a meteor hit Earth, breaking off a piece of crust that shot thousands of miles upward....

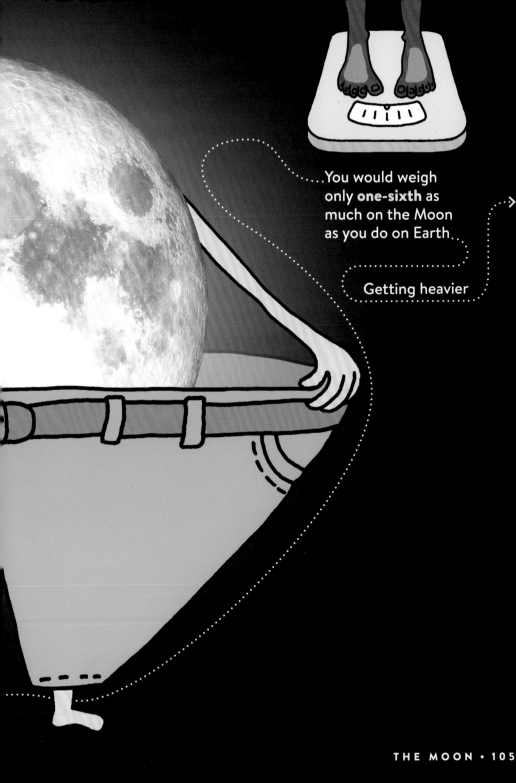

You would weigh only **one-sixth** as much on the Moon as you do on Earth.

Getting heavier

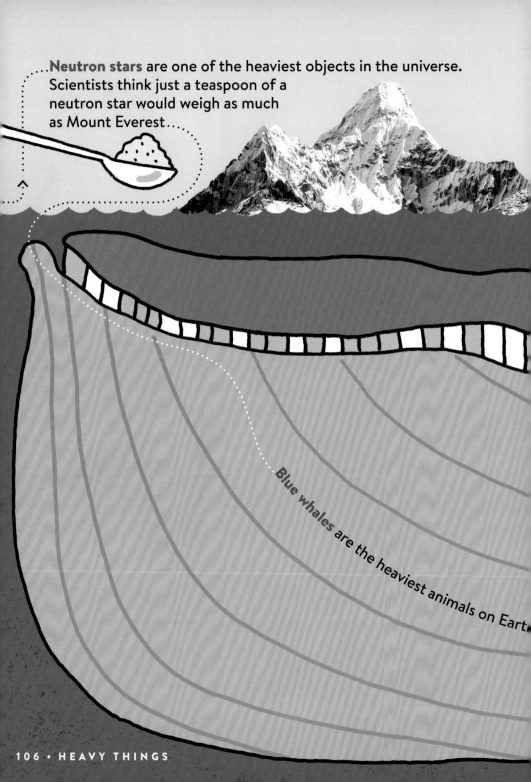

Neutron stars are one of the heaviest objects in the universe. Scientists think just a teaspoon of a neutron star would weigh as much as Mount Everest...

Blue whales are the heaviest animals on Earth.

Lighten up!

A newborn gains 200 pounds (91kg) every day during its first year

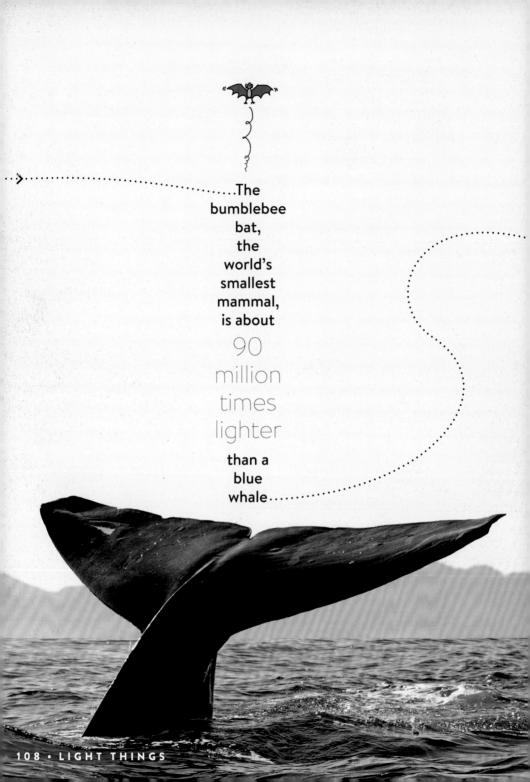

The bumblebee bat, the world's smallest mammal, is about

90 million times lighter

than a blue whale

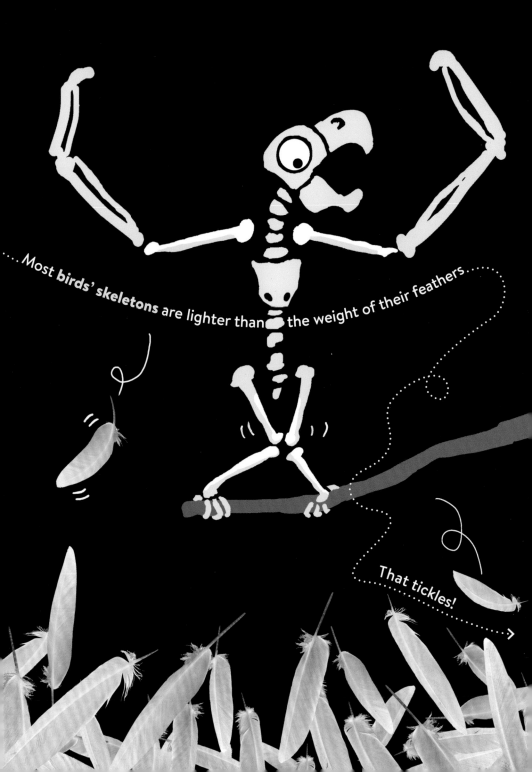

Most birds' skeletons are lighter than the weight of their feathers

That tickles!

Woodpeckers have special feathers on their **nostrils** to prevent them from accidentally breathing in wood chips as they drum on trees.

More feathery friends

Go to page 72

Some birds make sounds using just their feathers in what's called **"wing singing"**

La-la-la

Baby flamingos aren't born with **pink feathers,** they're white or gray.

When singing in a group, choir members' **heart** rates can synchronize.

There's an ice field shaped like a **heart** on **Pluto**.

Hairy frogs can break their own **bones** in their hands and feet and push the shards out through their skin, creating a defensive **claw**.

Sharks don't have **bones**.

The force from the pinch of a coconut crab's **claws** is nearly as strong as a **lion's** bite.

Lions can **sleep** up to 20 hours a day.

Pluto is named after the **Roman** god of the underworld.

Ancient **Romans** would whiten their **teeth** with pee.

Dragonfish **teeth** are see-through and stronger than those of a great white **shark**.

Some animals can **sleep** standing up—horses, flamingos, and elephants among them.

An elephant in the room

Elephants communicate using sounds in frequencies too low for humans to hear. The sounds **vibrate through the ground**, and elephants use their **feet and trunks** to "listen" to them.

Listen up!

Ring-tailed lemurs on Madagascar use " **Hmmm** " sounds to call out to their friends.

Parasaurolophus was a dinosaur with a bony crest on its head that it might have used like a **TRUMPET** to call to other dinosaurs in its herd...

Making music

The sound from the Great Stalacpipe Organ, located in a cave in Virginia, comes from **cave stalactites**.

Turn it up!

↑
Go to page 90

More record-setters

The sound of **icebergs cracking** can be so loud that scientists sometimes pick it up with microphones at the equator

A man in the U.K. holds the world record for the loudest

BURP.

His nickname is "The Burper King."

Howler monkey calls are so loud they can be heard up to 3 miles (4.8km) away

The **clicking sounds** that a sperm whale makes can be as loud as a rocket ship at takeoff

At the right frequency,

a singer

can sing loud enough to break glass.

Shhhh!

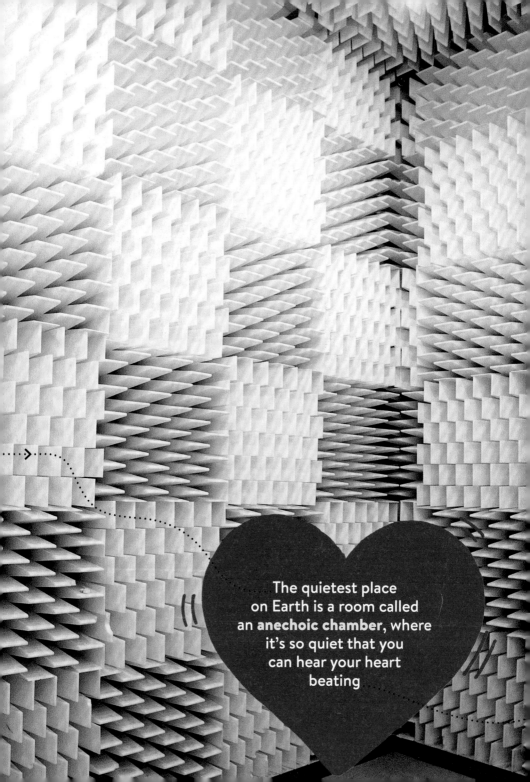

The quietest place on Earth is a room called **an anechoic chamber**, where it's so quiet that you can hear your heart beating

Go to page 84

Flying high

The design of an **owl's feathers** allows it to fly almost silently. Experts are studying owl wings in the hopes of making quieter airplanes and wind turbines.

There is sound in **outer space**, but humans can't hear it.

At night, giraffes quietly **hum** to one another.

Autonomous sensory meridian response (ASMR) is the term for the **tingling feeling** that some people experience in response to **certain sensations** and sounds, like tapping fingers, crinkling paper, or whispers.

Quiet, please

QUIET THINGS • 123

At two libraries in Portugal, bats live among the bookshelves, **eating bugs** that could damage the books.

The two lion statues that guard the steps of the New York Public Library are more than 100 years old and are named Patience and Fortitude.

Roooaar!

A pride of lions succeeds on their **hunts** only about 30 percent of the time......

Sekhmet, the ancient Egyptian **goddess of war**, was often depicted with the head of a lioness....

People who are **allergic** to pet cats are likely **allergic to lions**, too....

Meowww!

Male lions aren't the only ones t

Go to page 34

Lions have excellent night vision—they can see six times better in the dark than people can.

row manes—female lions can grow them, too.

Good hair day

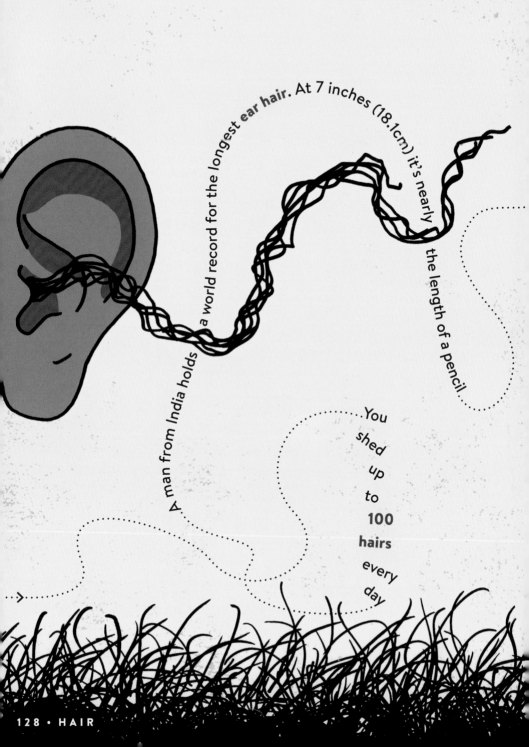

A man from India holds a world record for the longest **ear hair**. At 7 inches (18.1cm) it's nearly the length of a pencil

You shed up to **100** hairs every day

At the World

BEARD AND
MOUSTACHE
Championships,
some competitors
style their facial hair
in wacky designs.

You're a winner!

Every year, a town in England hosts a **worm-charming** contest. Contestants try to coax as many worms as they can out of the ground by sticking a rod or a garden fork in the dirt and making it vibrate.

Wriggle away!

Earthworm eggs look like mini **lemons**.

You can use **lemons** to power a **light bulb**.

When Thomas Edison was working on the **light bulb**, he tested more than a thousand materials for the filament, or wire, inside—even beard **hair**.

Off the coast of Japan, there's an **island** where **cats** outnumber humans.

Stubbs the **cat** was elected honorary mayor of a small town in **Alaska**.

There's a species of **pink** iguana that's found on only one **island** on Earth.

Alaska holds the world's largest outhouse race every year. According to the rules, every outhouse must have a roll of toilet **paper** inside.

Instead of toilet **paper**, the Romans wiped using a stick with a **sponge** on the end.

Some food companies use a chemical made from human **hair** in **pizza** dough.

Pizza has been delivered to the **International Space Station**.

Scientists have discovered a **planet** covered in **pink** gas.

For parts of the year, there are three **sunrises** on **planet** HD 131399Ab because it orbits three different suns.

Astronauts aboard the **International Space Station** see 16 **sunrises** and sunsets every day.

Show your moves!

Ocean creatures called glass **sponges** grow intricate skeletons that look like glass. Sometimes **shrimp** live inside them.

Some species of cleaner **shrimp** dance to attract fish.

Each morning, seahorse pairs "dance" together to reinforce their bond

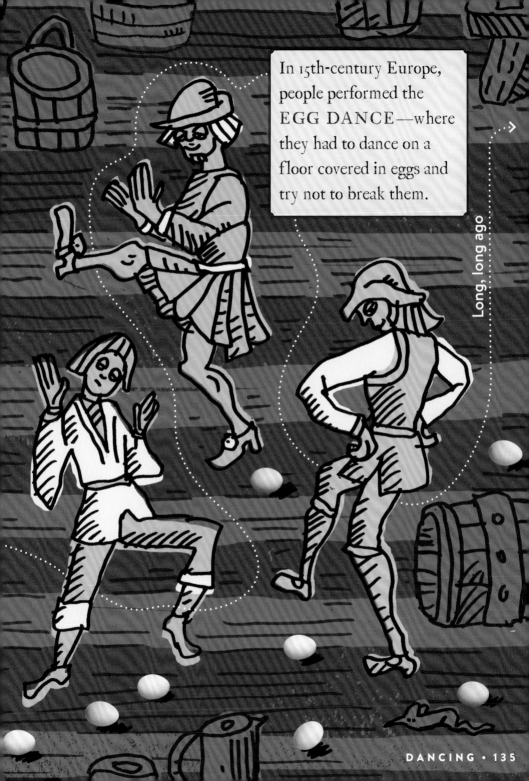

In 15th-century Europe, people performed the **EGG DANCE**—where they had to dance on a floor covered in eggs and try not to break them.

Long, long ago

Go to page 106

....A field in Laos, in Southeast Asia, is covered with hundreds of **ancient stone jars**. Some are 10 feet (3m) tall and weigh as much as two elephants ....

Heave-ho!

Mysterious 12-sided **bronze objects** that date back to ancient Rome have turned up across northern Europe—they could be toys, tools to measure distance, or even candlesticks.

The stone ball that rolls after Indiana Jones in the movie Raiders of the Lost Ark is inspired by hundreds of heavy boulders chiseled smooth by ancient inhabitants of Costa Rica.

So shapely

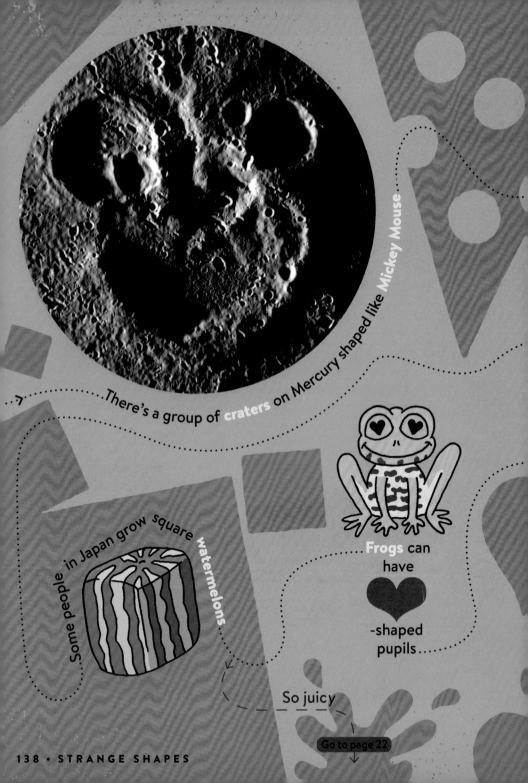

There's a group of **craters** on Mercury shaped like *Mickey Mouse*

Some people in Japan grow square **watermelons**

Frogs can have ♥-shaped pupils

So juicy

Go to page 22

Go to page 166

More on planets

Follow the trunk!

...In Germany, there's a **school** shaped like a cat.

There's a **skyscraper** in Bangkok, Thailand, shaped like an elephant...

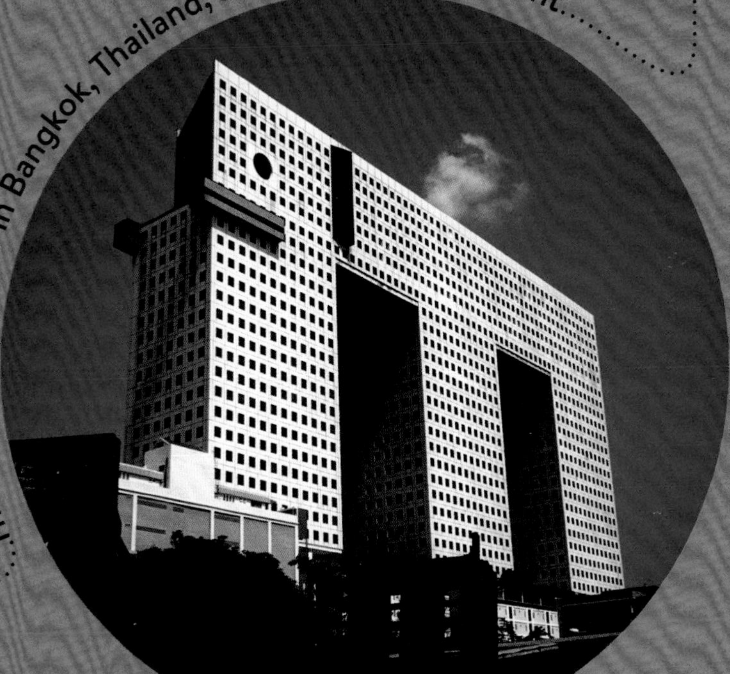

Rrribbit!

Go to page 170

An elephant's trunk is strong enough to push over a **tree**.

Cow stomachs have **four** compartments.

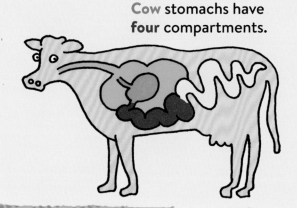

There are **four** tentacles on a **slug**'s head. It uses the two on top to smell and see and the bottom two to feel and taste.

Some **slugs** protect themselves by producing **sticky**, glue-like slime, so that predators can't lift them off the surface they're on.

There's a **tree** called a **rainbow** eucalyptus that has multi-colored bark.

Scientists think **rainbows** appear on Saturn's moon **Titan**.

Titan has a sea made of liquid **methane**.

Methane gas is what **cow** burps are made of.

A **sticky** mucus that's 400 times thicker than human spit covers the tip of a chameleon's **tongue**.

The okapi, a hoofed mammal that lives in the African rainforest and is related to giraffes, can use its long **tongue** to clean its ears.

What's that?

One man in the U.K. can pull an entire

double decker

bus with his ears.......

It's heating up

Jackrabbits use their huge ears to help release body heat and **keep cool** in the desert

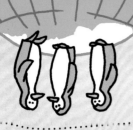

Go to page 50

Second skin

Thorny devils, desert-dwelling lizards from **Australia**, use their skin **like a straw** to suck in water from sand and transport it directly to the lizard's mouth like a drink...

Not all deserts are hot. The world's largest desert is in **Antarctica**, where temperatures can drop below -128°F (-89°C).

There's a hole in a desert in **Turkmenistan** that **contains a** **fire** that's been burning for more than 50 years...

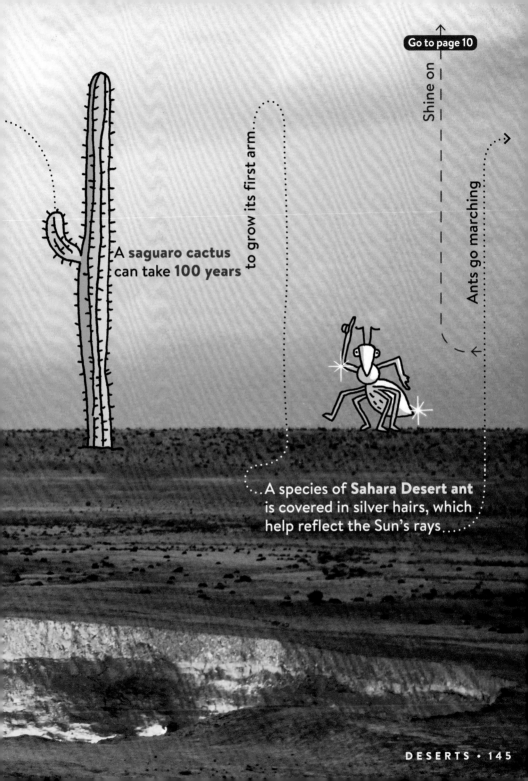

Go to page 10

Shine on

Ants go marching

A **saguaro cactus** can take **100 years** to grow its first arm.

A species of **Sahara Desert ant** is covered in silver hairs, which help reflect the Sun's rays.

Ants have been around since
the time of the dinosaurs.

If there's a flood, a colony of fire ants can **form a raft** and float for weeks until they reach safety.

All aboard!

Boaters at one race in Canada paddle in giant, hollowed-out pumpkins

Under the waves

About three million **shipwrecks** are scattered across the ocean floor

Go to page 40

According to legend, bringing a banana on a boat is bad luck

Banana-tastic!

Scientists have done studies to show how **SLippery** banana peels are.

Banana plants aren't trees— they're an **herb** related to ginger.

Bananas are naturally **radioactive**— but you'd have to eat at least a billion in one meal to consume a deadly dose

A single banana is called a **finger**, while a group of bananas is called a **hand**.

Let's celebrate!

Banana Split Day is celebrated in the U.S.A. in August

During the Christmas season in Iceland, the Yule Lads put either candy or rotten potatoes in your shoes...

Sweetly does it!

One of
the inventors
of the

cotton candy

machine
was a dentist.

↑
Go to page 102

Find some space!

..........Sugar used to be prescribed as **medicine**....

M&Ms were the first candies eaten **in space**...

:..Archaeologists have found **chewing gum** that's 5,700 years old....

Crushing **sugar crystals** can create static electricity

Such a shock!

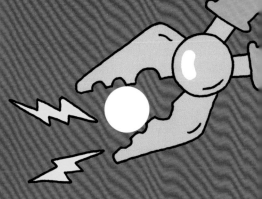

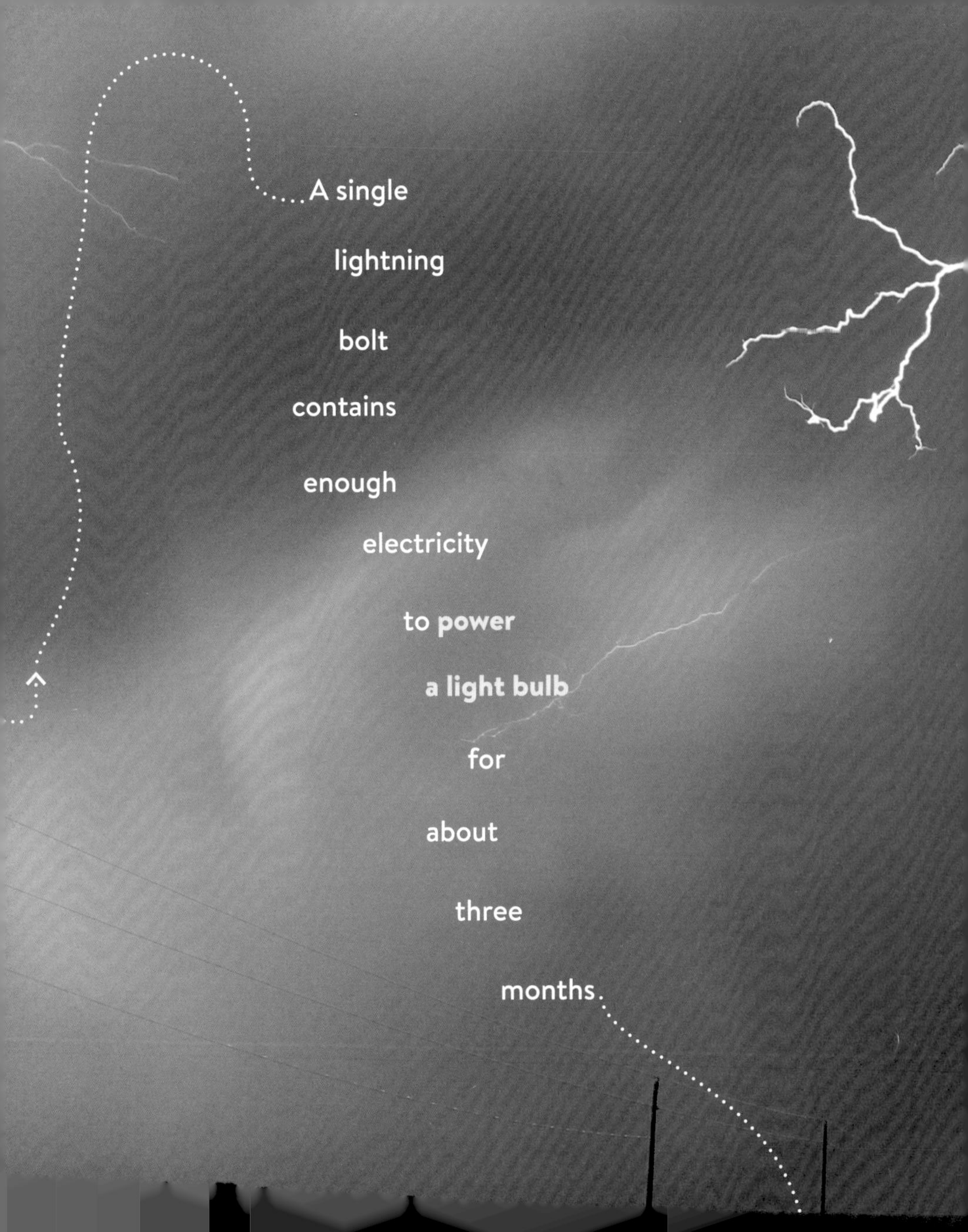

A single

lightning

bolt

contains

enough

electricity

to power

a light bulb

for

about

three

months.

Storms ahead

Erupting **VOLCANOES** can create lightning.

Ball lightning is an electric floating bubble that has been known to break through windows.

Scientists think that lightning **strikes** helped early life evolve.

THE EMPIRE STATE BUILDING IN NEW YORK CITY IS HIT BY LIGHTNING ABOUT 25 TIMES A YEAR.

The "lightning capital of the world" is a lake in Venezuela where lightning **storms** occur nearly 300 days of the year.

Splash!

There's a park in **Austria** that each year floods and turns into a lake, submerging trails, benches, and even bridges....

Canada's Kliluk, nicknamed **Spotted Lake**, partially dries in the summer and reveals hundreds of colorful mineral pools that, from above, look like spots.

Off to the park!

On the world's fastest rollercoaster, at an amusement park in Abu Dhabi, passengers wear goggles t

At Crater of Diamonds State Park in Arkansas, you can keep any rocks or gemstones you find—visitors have discovered more than **75,000 diamonds** there.

So precious

Diggerland is a theme park where visitors can **drive trucks and backhoes**, and go on other construction-themed rides.

...thstand zooming along at nearly 150 miles an hour (240km/h)

Scientists think that there are opals on Mars.

One of the **largest emeralds** ever discovered weighs as much as three giant pandas.

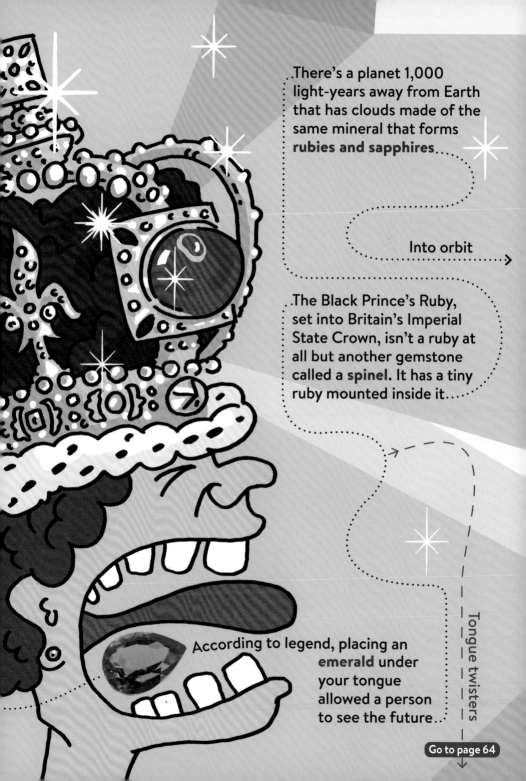

There's a planet 1,000 light-years away from Earth that has clouds made of the same mineral that forms **rubies and sapphires**.

Into orbit →

The Black Prince's Ruby, set into Britain's Imperial State Crown, isn't a ruby at all but another gemstone called a **spinel**. It has a tiny ruby mounted inside it.

According to legend, placing an **emerald** under your tongue allowed a person to see the future.

Tongue twisters

Go to page 64

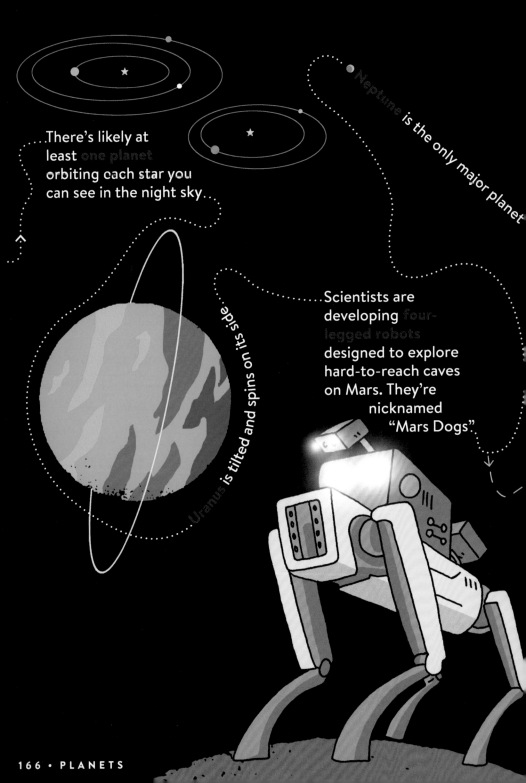

There's likely at least one planet orbiting each star you can see in the night sky.

Neptune is the only major planet

Scientists are developing four-legged robots designed to explore hard-to-reach caves on Mars. They're nicknamed "Mars Dogs".

Uranus is tilted and spins on its side

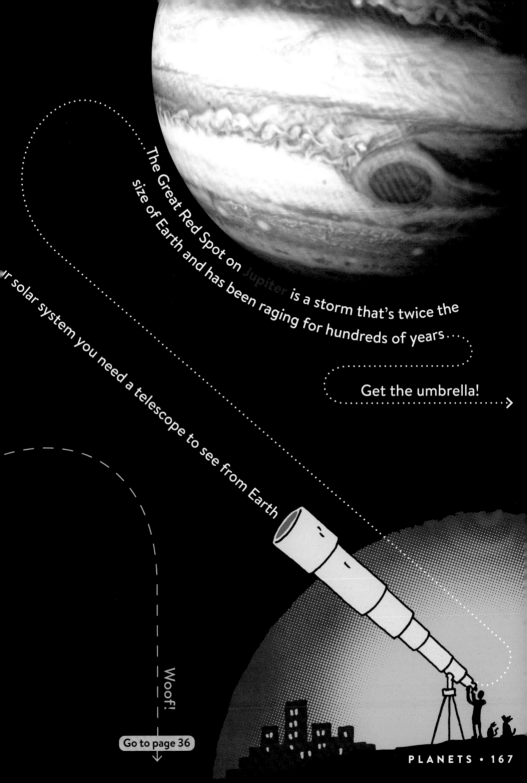

The Great Red Spot on Jupiter is a storm that's twice the size of Earth and has been raging for hundreds of years....

Get the umbrella! ⟶

r solar system you need a telescope to see from Earth

Woof!

Go to page 36

Sometimes it rains animals. There have been reports since ancient times of it raining bats, fish, and even frogs. This happens when animals are picked up by tornadoes or waterspouts and dropped elsewhere.

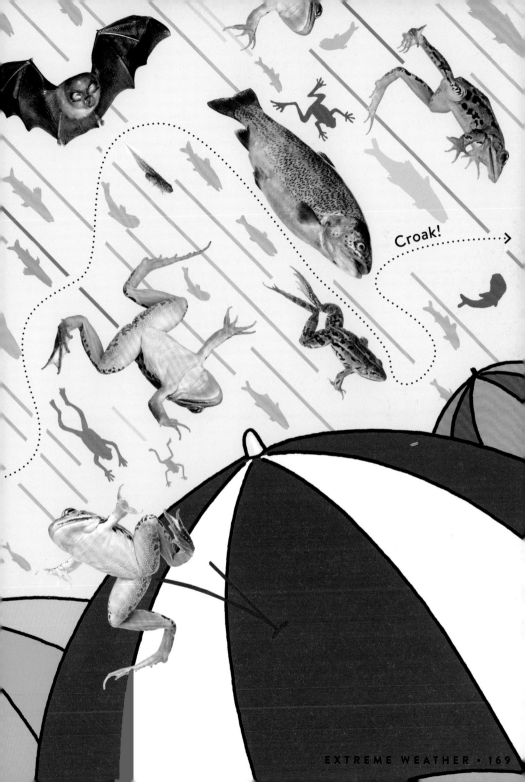

Croak!

There's one species of tree frog that's completely **see-through**—you can see its heart beating and its food being digested

Though all **toads** are frogs, not all frogs are toads

A group of frogs is sometimes called an

ARMY

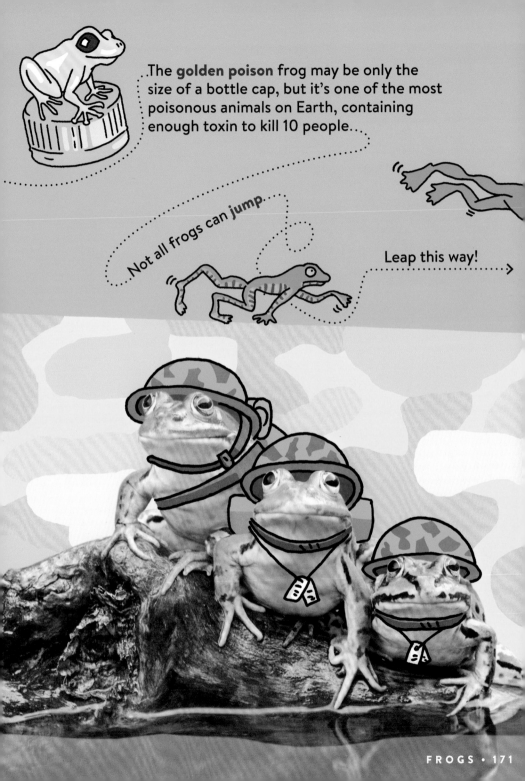

The **golden poison** frog may be only the size of a bottle cap, but it's one of the most poisonous animals on Earth, containing enough toxin to kill 10 people...

Not all frogs can jump.

Leap this way! →

·····> A jumping **spider** can leap up to 40 times its own body length—the same as a person being able to hop the length of three tennis courts at once.

Mexican jumping beans are actually **seed pods** with a moth larva inside— when the seeds are warm, the baby moth moves around causing the seed to " JUMP "

Marvelous moths

There's a species of South American moth that drinks tears from **birds** while they sleep.

Hoatzins are **birds** whose chicks are born with claws on their wings. They use them to climb **trees**.

Lawnmower racing is a **sport** in the U.S.A. The fastest models can zoom at speeds of 150 miles an hour (241km/h).

In the **sport** of **toe** wrestling, opponents try to pin down each other's foot.

Bacteria from between people's **toes** has been used to make **cheese**.

The world's most expensive **cheese**, called *pule*, is made from donkey **milk**.

The tropical manchineel **tree** is incredibly **poisonous**—the Spanish name for its fruit means "little apple of death."

Eels have **poisonous blood.**

A male **ostrich** makes a call that sounds like a lion's **roar**.

Around three drops of human **blood** can have about one billion red blood **cells**.

A tiger can **roar** 25 times louder than the sound of a **lawnmower**.

The largest single **cell** on Earth is the yolk of an **ostrich** egg—which is 25 times more massive than a chicken egg.

A **cockroach** can survive for weeks without its head—it doesn't need its **brain** in order to breathe.

The **milk** from one species of **cockroach** is the most nutritious substance on Earth. Scientists are studying it to make foods of the future.

Some animals have more than one **brain**—octopuses have nine.

More octo-facts

Some octopuses can temporarily change their **skin texture** from **smooth** to *spiny*

Octopuses have *no bones* so they're able to fit in very small spaces. A 600-pound (272kg) octopus can fit through a hole smaller than a walnut

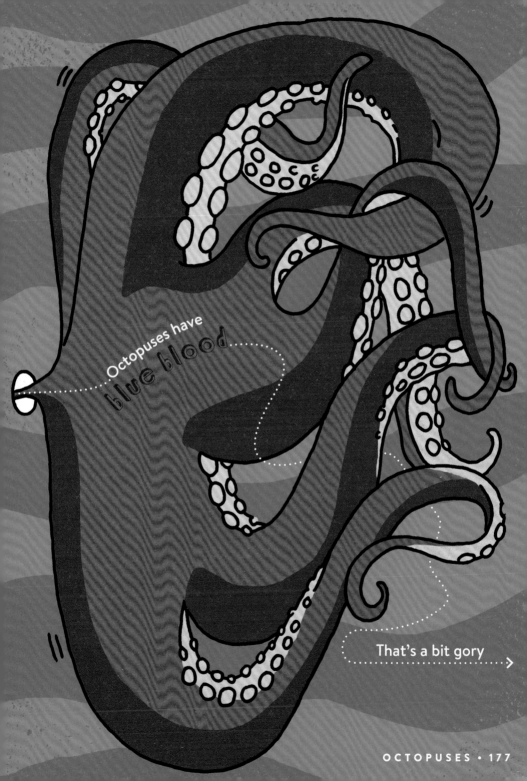

Octopuses have
blue blood

That's a bit gory →

Vampire ground finches **drink the blood** of other birds.

More brilliant birds

Go to page 72

Blood Falls is a **red waterfall** that runs off an Antarctic glacier. It gets its blood-red color from iron in the water.

Look out!

Some athletes climb **frozen** waterfalls.

An artist created a waterfall sculpture made out of about **10,000 toilet bowls**.

Sooooo tall

Niagara Falls drew daredevils to perform stunts in the early 1900s. The first person to go over Niagara Falls in a **barrel** was a schoolteacher.

The **tallest waterfall** in the world is Angel Falls in Venezuela—it's taller than three **Eiffel Towers** stacked on top of one another.

Scientists classify waterfalls into different **categories such as chutes, fans, cascades, and punchbowls**.

One of the tallest snowpeople ever built was so big it had trees for arms and truck tires for buttons

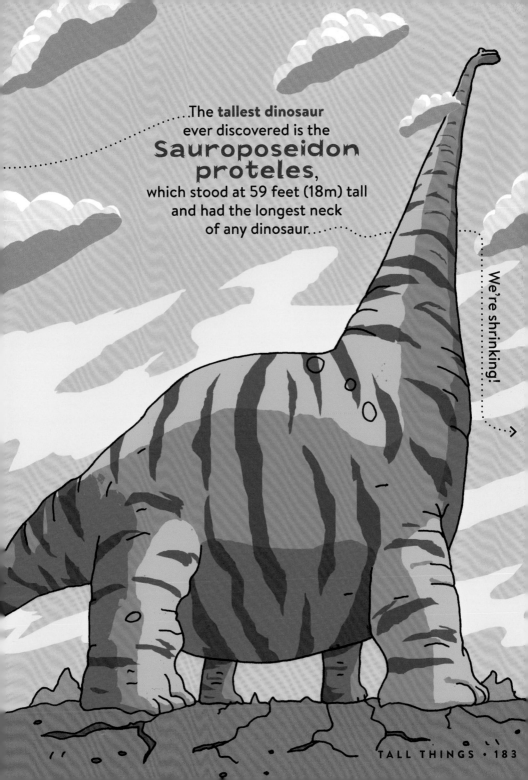

The **tallest dinosaur** ever discovered is the **Sauroposeidon proteles,** which stood at 59 feet (18m) tall and had the longest neck of any dinosaur.

We're shrinking!

The planet Kepler-78b has only an 8.5-hour year.

The world's shortest dog, Milly the Chihuahua, is only 3.8 inches (9.65cm) tall—as a newborn, she could fit **in a teaspoon**.........

Aww...baby

Newborn **giraffes** can stand up just 30 minutes after they're born.

The only country in the world that doesn't have a **flag** shaped like a rectangle is **Nepal**.

Only two countries today have the color **purple** in their national **flag**: Nicaragua and Dominica.

Giraffes have **purple** tongues.

Legend says **Nepal** is home to the yeti, also known as the Abominable **Snowman**.

Getting cloudy ····················>

A **snowman** was once sculpted by famous Renaissance **artist** Michelangelo.

Trees in the Amazon **rainforest** make their own rain clouds.

Artists' brains are structured differently from those of non-artists.

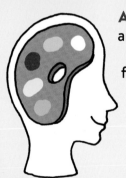

Goliath birdeaters are **spiders** that live in the **rainforest** and can grow as big as puppies.

The **brains** of some **spiders** extend into their legs.

Noctilucent clouds form about 50 miles (80km) above Earth's surface. Experts think they're made out of *ice crystals* that have formed on meteor dust

Lenticular clouds often look like **UFOs**.

Nice hat! ›

A cloud that forms on top of a **mountain** peak is sometimes called a cap cloud.

Some of the stone statues on Easter Island have red hats made of **volcanic rock**. Called *pukao*, these hats can weigh as much as three rhinos.

U.S. President Abraham Lincoln kept important papers in his **stovepipe** top hat.

Scientists outfit seals with special hats that contain high-tech sensors to help study Earth's climate.

Go to page 106

Weigh up these facts

Protect yourself f'

A **knight's helmet**
could weigh as much as 8 pounds (4kg)—
as heavy as a cat

It's said that the 100
folds in a **chef's hat**
represent all the ways
you can cook an egg

Knights in the
Middle Ages
put armor, called barding,
on war horses

Ride on!

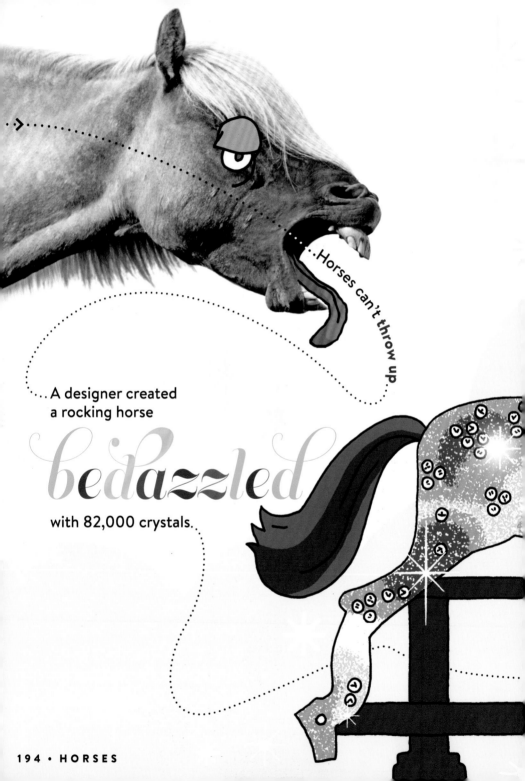

Horses can't throw up.

A designer created a rocking horse *bedazzled* with 82,000 crystals.

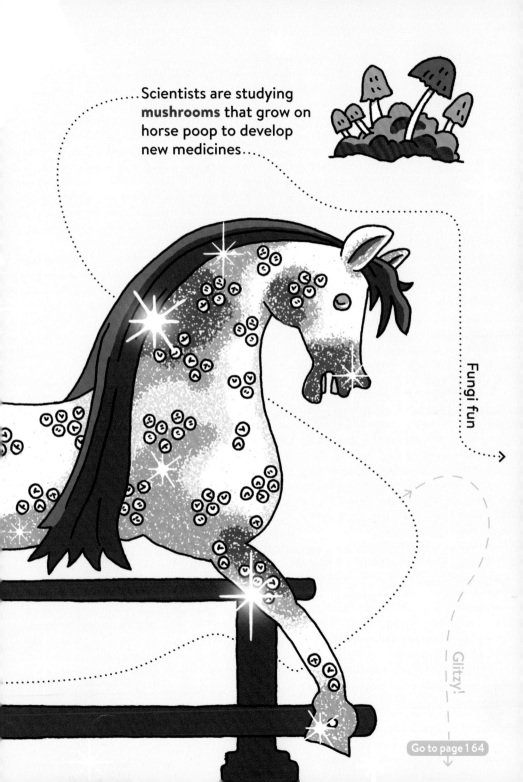

Scientists are studying **mushrooms** that grow on horse poop to develop new medicines...

Fungi fun

Glitzy!

Go to page 164

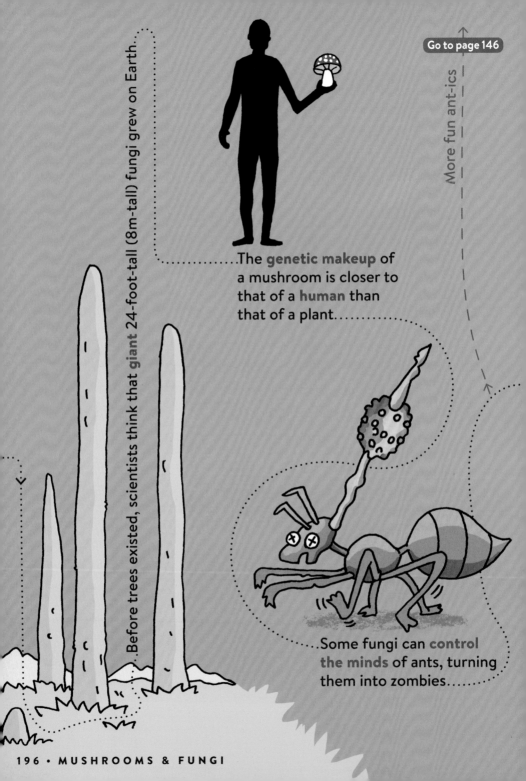

Go to page 146

More fun ant-ics

The **genetic makeup** of a mushroom is closer to that of a **human** than that of a plant.

Before trees existed, scientists think that giant 24-foot-tall (8m-tall) fungi grew on Earth.

Some fungi can **control the minds** of ants, turning them into zombies.

Trees use a network of fungi to **communicate** with one another, in what is termed the Wood Wide Web.

Some mushrooms

glow

in the dark.

Lights out! ⟩

Tarsiers, a type of primate, can see in full color even in near darkness. The animal has excellent night vision because each eye is enormous—even bigger than its brain.

Index

Meet the FACTopians

Kate Hale is an author, editor, and professional fun-fact finder based in Alexandria, Virginia. A former editor for National Geographic Kids, Kate has edited or written about everything from how dogs communicate to biographies of inspiring scientists. When researching more facts to include in *Return to FACTopia*, Kate made sure to include all the awesome info she couldn't fit in the first book. And now every time she sees a shooting star, she'll wonder if it's actually astronaut poop that's been ejected from the International Space Station.

Andy Smith is an award-winning illustrator. A graduate of the Royal College of Art, London, U.K., he creates artwork that has an optimistic, handmade feel. Creating the illustrations for *Return to FACTopia* has brought even more surprises, from zombie ants to vegetable orchestras! Andy's favorite fact is that some 1950s movie theaters piped scents under the audience's seats—he thinks it's about time that Smell-O-Vision made a comeback.

Lawrence Morton is an art director and designer based in London, U.K. He created a trail of dots through the pages to help the reader navigate safely as they embark on their *Return to FACTopia*. The frozen waterfall brought back happy memories of climbing mountains in Scotland and the Alps, wielding an ice pick with crampons strapped to his boots.

Sources

Scientists and other experts are discovering new facts and updating information all the time. That's why our *FACTopia* team has checked that every fact that appears in this book is based on multiple trustworthy sources and has been verified by the Britannica team. Of the hundreds of sources used in this book, here is a list of key websites we consulted.

News Organizations
abcnews.go.com
theatlantic.com
bbc.com
bbc.co.uk
cbc.ca
cbsnews.com
cnn.com
cntraveler.com
theguardian.com
kids.nationalgeographic.com
nationalgeographic.com
nationalgeographic.org
nbcnews.com
npr.org
nytimes.com
reuters.com
sciencefocus.com
scientificamerican.com
slate.com
time.com
travelandleisure.com
washingtonpost.com
wired.com
usatoday.com
vice.com
vox.com

Government, Scientific, and Academic Organizations
audubon.org
academic.eb.com
britannica.com

jstor.org
loc.gov
merriam-webster.com
nature.com
nasa.gov
ncbi.nlm.nih.gov
noaa.gov
royalsocietypublishing.org
sciencedirect.com
sciencemag.org

Museums and Zoos
amnh.org
animals.sandiegozoo.org
askdruniverse.wsu.edu
floridamuseum.ufl.edu
kids.sandiegozoo.org
nationalzoo.si.edu
metmuseum.org
nhm.ac.uk
ocean.si.edu
si.edu
smithsonianmag.com

Universities
animaldiversity.org
harvard.edu
illinois.edu
stanford.edu
washington.edu

Other Websites
akc.org
atlasobscura.com
dkfindout.com
guinnessworldrecords.com
nwf.org
pbs.org
ripleys.com
sciencedaily.com
snopes.com
worldwildlife.org

Picture Credits

The publisher would like to thank the following for permission to reproduce their photographs and illustrations. While every effort has been made to credit images, the publisher apologizes for any errors or omissions and will be pleased to make any necessary corrections in future editions of the book.

t = top; l = left; r = right; c = center; b = bottom

Cover Images: Front tr by _nicholas/iStockphoto; Front bl Mats Silvan/Getty Images; Back 3DSculptor/iStockphoto.

p.2 Leblanc Catherine/Alamy; p.6 Peter Horree/Alamy; pp.8–9 Westend61/Getty Images; pp.10–11 Rawan Hussein/123rf.com; pp.12–13 golf was here/Getty Images; pp.14–15 Michael Runkel/robertharding/Getty Images; p.18 Geng Xu/500px/Getty Images; p.20 Minden Pictures/Alamy; p.23 antpkr/iStockphoto; p.24t Pat Canova/Alamy; p.24b Sean Gallup/Getty Images; p.29 Phichaklim2/iStockphoto; p.30 andreykuzmin/123rf.com; p.31 Reuters/Alamy; pp.32–33 Michael Ventura/Alamy; p.34 Akimasa Harada/Getty Images; pp.36–37 Tim Platt/Getty Images; pp.38–39 DieterMeyrl/Getty Images; p.43 NASA; pp.44–45 David Marano Photography/Getty Images; p.46 Andrew Whitehead/Alamy; p.49c Daniel Timothy Allison/123rf.com; p.49b Image Source/Alamy; pp.50–51 PicturePartners/iStockphoto; p.52 Biosphoto/Alamy; p.55 ullstein bild/Getty Images; pp.56–57 Jasmin Merdan/Getty Images; p.58 Blue Planet Archive/Alamy; p.60 Andrew Mackay/Alamy; pp.62–63 Lew Robertson/Getty Images; p.65 Antonio Guillem/Dreamstime; pp.68–69 Dominque Braud/Dembinsky Photo Associates/Alamy; p.70 Mathieu Meur/Stocktrek Images/Getty Images; p.73 wilpunt/Getty Images; p.74 Jaana Pesonen/Shutterstock; p.75 3DSculptor/iStockphoto; p.77 Jonathan Knowles/Getty Images; p.79 Image by Marie LaFauci/Getty Images; pp.80–81 Andrija Majsen/Alamy; p.82 Anip Shah/Getty Images; p.85 Андрей Елкин/iStockphoto; pp.86–87 Sabena Jane Blackbird/Alamy; p.88 Tanes Ngamsom/iStockphoto; p.90 Atthapon Kulpakdeesingworn/Alamy; p.91 by_nicholas/iStockphoto; p.92tl The Print Collector/Alamy; p.92tr claudiodivizia/iStockphoto; p.93cr claudiodivizia/iStockphoto; p.94 Willem Kolvoort/Nature Picture Library; pp.96–97 Leonello Calvetti/Getty Images; p.99 Alpha Historical/Alamy; p.100 Reuters/Alamy; p.101 jirkaejc/123rf.com; p.102 Peter Horree/Alamy; p.104 Science History Images/Alamy; pp.104–105 NASA; p.106 John Philip Harper/Getty Images; p.108 VW Pics/Getty Images; p.109 MirageC/Getty Images; p.111 anankkmi/iStockphoto; p.112 NASA; pp.114–115 Lisa Mckelvie/Getty Images; p.116 Vrabelpeter1/Dreamstime; p.118 Mint Images/Getty Images; p.119 Brad Calkins/Dreamstime; p.121 Stephen Rudolph/Dreamstime; p.122 Sueddeutsche Zeitung Photo/Alamy; pp.124–125 Hemis/Alamy; p.126 Isselee/Dreamstime; p.129 JohnnyGreig/iStockphoto; p.129 Yuri_Arcurs/iStockphoto; pp.130–131 PA Images/Alamy; p.133 David Shale/Nature Picture Library; pp.134–135 Bozena_Fulawka/iStockphoto; pp.136–137 agefotostock/Alamy; p.138 NASA; p.139 Shaun Higson/Thailand—Bangkok/Alamy; p.141 Danita Delimont/Getty Images; p.143 Bryce Flynn/Getty Images; pp.144–145 Tim Whitby/Alamy; pp.146–147 SonerCdem/iStockphoto; pp.148–149 Damocean/iStockphoto; p.151 Harvey Tsoi/Getty Images; p.153tl Milos Tasic/Dreamstime; p.153tr Djama86/Dreamstime; p.153cl Anke Van Wyk/Dreamstime; p.153cr Barelkodotcom/Dreamstime; p.153bl Primaveraar/Dreamstime; p.153br pepifoto/iStockphoto; p.154 Pomah/Dreamstime; pp.156–157 Vincent Marquez/EyeEm/Getty Images; p.159 Mauritius images GmbH/Alamy; pp.160–161 Westend61/Getty Images; p.162 Leblanc Catherine/Alamy; p.164 Andy Koehler/123rf.com; p.165 lermannika/iStockphoto; p.167 NASA; p.168 PaulPaladin/iStockphoto (carp); p.168 blickwinkel/Alamy (bat); p.168 Nature Photographers Ltd/Alamy (frog); pp.168–169 Isselee/Dreamstime (frogs); pp.168–169 Edd Westmacott/Alamy (trout); p.169 blickwinkel/Alamy (bat); pp.170–171 Rolf Nussbaumer Photography/Alamy; pp.172–173 pungem/iStockphoto; p.174 Bloomberg/Getty Images; p.178 Donyanedomam/iStockphoto; p.180 Daniel Milchev/Getty Images; p.184 PandorumBS/Alamy; p.185 -slav-/iStockphoto; p.186 travel4pictures/Alamy; p.187 dpa picture alliance/Alamy; pp.188–189 Arsty/iStockphoto; p.190 Paul Grace Photography Somersham/Getty Images; p.191 Mats Silvan/Getty Images; pp.192–193 Petra Tänzer/EyeEm/Getty Images; p.194 WILDLIFE GmbH/Alamy; p.197 Anna Stowe Landscapes UK/Alamy.

BRITANNICA
BOOKS

Britannica Books is an imprint of What on Earth Publishing,
published in collaboration with Britannica, Inc.
Allington Castle, Maidstone, Kent ME16 0NB, United Kingdom
30 Ridge Road Unit B, Greenbelt, Maryland, 20770, United States

First published in the United States in 2022

Written by Kate Hale
Illustrated by Andy Smith
Designed by Lawrence Morton
Edited by Judy Barratt
Indexed by Vanessa Bird

Encyclopaedia Britannica
Alison Eldridge, Managing Editor; Michele Rita Metych, Fact-checking Supervisor

Britannica Books
Nancy Feresten, Publisher; Natalie Bellos, Executive Editor; Meg Osborne, Assistant Editor;
Andy Forshaw, Art Director; Alenka Oblak, Production Manager

Library of Congress Cataloging-in-Publication Data available upon request

ISBN: 9781913750404

Printed in India

1 3 5 7 9 10 8 6 4 2

whatonearthbooks.com
books.britannica.com

MIX
Paper from
responsible sources
FSC® C016779

Think.
Seek.
Play.
Learn.
Britannica.

Your family's key to discovering the amazingly weird and strangely true.

Or visit
premium.britannica.com/learn